Mastering
Sales Managerial
Skills

Building High-Performing Teams & Driving Exceptional Results

Gerard Assey

Mastering Sales Managerial Skills:

Building High-Performing Teams & Driving Exceptional Results

By
Gerard Assey

Published by:
Gerard Assey
19/18, Palli Arasan Street
Anna Nagar East
Chennai - 600 102

ISBN: 978-93-92492-94-5

(Image courtesy Freepik: 'https://www.freepik.com' Thank You)

Table of Contents

- ✓ Personal Development for Sales Managers
- ✓ A Detailed Action Plan for Sales Managers to put these Skills into Practice
- ✓ Templates and Resources for Sales Planning, Performance Evaluation, and More
- ✓ Conclusion
- ✓ About the Author

Preface

In today's fast-paced and competitive business landscape, the role of a Sales Manager has never been more critical. Sales managers are the linchpin of success for any organization, responsible for driving revenue, managing teams, and ensuring that sales targets are not just met but exceeded.

This book, '**Mastering Sales Managerial Skills**: ***Building High-Performing Teams & Driving Exceptional*** *Results'* is designed as a valuable resource for both aspiring and seasoned Sales Managers. It delves deep into the multifaceted world of sales management, providing insights, strategies, and actionable steps to excel in this pivotal role.

Our journey through these pages will take you on a transformative path, one that empowers you to evolve as a leader, a strategist, and a mentor. Whether you're a mid-level manager looking to sharpen your skills or an organization seeking to equip your sales leaders with the tools they need, this book is your compass.

Throughout these chapters, you'll find a treasure trove of knowledge, from the fundamentals of leadership to the intricacies of sales strategy and the nuances of building lasting customer relationships. We've taken care to include real-world examples, detailed action plans, and strategies that you can implement immediately to make a tangible impact on your team's performance.

Our belief is simple: the success of a Sales Manager is not just about numbers but about fostering a culture of growth, professionalism, and innovation within the team. It's about setting a course for your

team's success and being adaptable in the face of change.
As we explore the various facets of sales management, we'll touch on everything from recruitment and training to goal-setting, performance management, data analytics, and ethical practices. We'll delve into the art of effective communication, conflict resolution, and time management. We'll journey through the landscape of customer relationship management, sales forecasting, budgeting, and even the critical areas of adapting to change and maintaining personal balance.
Each chapter is crafted with your growth in mind. We want you not just to read but to engage, to reflect, and to act. The comprehensive case studies and success stories woven throughout these pages will offer inspiration and insights from top-performing sales managers. They are living proof that the strategies outlined here can lead to remarkable achievements.
In the fast-evolving world of sales, your commitment to learning and development will be your greatest asset. Embrace the challenges, seize the opportunities, and continue your journey toward becoming an exceptional Sales Manager. Your success is not just a destination; it's a continuous path of improvement and achievement.

So, with an open mind and a thirst for knowledge, let's embark on this journey together.

May this book empower you to reach new heights as a Sales Manager, making an indelible mark on your team's success and contributing to the growth and prosperity of your organization.

Importance of this Book

Sales management plays a pivotal role in the success of any organization. At its core, it's the driving force behind achieving organizational goals, increasing revenue, and sustaining growth. Whether you're a seasoned sales manager looking to refine your skills or a budding leader ready to take the next step, this book, '**Mastering Sales Managerial Skills**: *Building High-Performing Teams & Driving Exceptional Results'* is designed to equip you with the knowledge, strategies, and practical tools needed to excel in the dynamic world of sales management.

The Importance of Sales Management

Imagine a company with a phenomenal product or service, one that could genuinely change lives or revolutionize industries. Without effective sales management, that company's potential might remain untapped. Sales managers are the linchpin between a company's offerings and its customers. They are the orchestrators of revenue generation, ensuring that the organization not only survives but thrives.

For instance, consider Company X, a tech startup with groundbreaking software. The engineers have created an innovative product, but it's the sales manager who takes this technology to the market, convinces customers of its value, and generates revenue to fund further development. Without adept sales management, the potential of Company X's product may never be realized.

Understanding the Target Audience

This book is primarily crafted for mid-level sales managers—those who have already gained some experience in sales and are ready to enhance their skills to propel their teams and organizations forward. You might be in a position where you've successfully led a sales team but want to refine your techniques, or you could be a sales representative aspiring to move up the ranks. Regardless of your current standing, the insights shared here are designed to be universally applicable.

For example, consider Jane, a mid-level sales manager at a regional pharmaceutical company. She's been successful in driving her team to meet quarterly targets consistently. However, she realizes that to take her career to the next level and lead a national team, she needs to fine-tune her managerial skills. This book will provide Jane with the tools and strategies she needs to make that leap.

The Purpose of This Book

The purpose of "Mastering Sales Managerial Skills" is to offer a comprehensive guide that covers every facet of sales management, from recruitment to performance measurement. It aims to bridge the gap between theory and practice, providing actionable steps and real-world examples to help you become a more effective and successful sales manager.

Throughout this book, you'll find not only concepts but also practical action plans and strategies that you can immediately apply to your role. Whether you're seeking to improve your team's performance, master the art of strategic planning, or navigate the complexities of ethical sales practices, each chapter is designed to provide you with the tools and knowledge needed to excel.

In the pages that follow, we'll embark on a journey through the world of sales management, exploring proven techniques, industry best practices, and the wisdom of experienced sales leaders. By the end, you'll be armed with the skills and insights necessary to not only manage a high-performing sales team but also drive exceptional results that contribute significantly to your organization's success. Welcome to the world of mastering sales managerial skills.

The Role of a Sales Manager

Sales management is a multifaceted role that serves as the bridge between an organization's products or services and its customers. In this chapter, we will delve into the fundamental aspects of the sales manager's role, responsibilities, and how it distinguishes itself from that of a sales representative.

Defining the Role and Responsibilities of a Sales Manager

A sales manager is the key driver behind the success of a sales team and, ultimately, the organization. Their primary responsibilities encompass:

- ✓ **Team Leadership**: Sales managers are responsible for assembling and leading a team of sales professionals. This involves recruiting, hiring, training, and motivating team members.

  Action Plan: Develop a recruitment strategy that identifies the right talent for your team. Create an onboarding program that integrates new hires smoothly into the team and organization. Establish regular team meetings to maintain open lines of communication.
- ✓ **Setting Goals and Targets**: Sales managers establish clear sales goals and targets for the team. They define what success looks like and communicate these objectives effectively.

  Action Plan: Implement the SMART (Specific, Measurable, Achievable, Relevant, Time-bound) framework to set precise goals. Break down targets into smaller, achievable milestones to keep the team motivated and on track.

- ✓ **Performance Evaluation**: Sales managers regularly assess the performance of their team members. This involves measuring against predefined metrics, offering feedback, and addressing areas that need improvement.
  Action Plan: Create a performance evaluation system that aligns with your team's goals and KPIs. Conduct regular one-on-one meetings with team members to provide constructive feedback and set development goals.
- ✓ **Strategic Planning**: They play a crucial role in developing sales strategies and plans. This includes identifying target markets, pricing strategies, and distribution channels.
  Action Plan: Develop a strategic planning process that involves market research, competitor analysis, and SWOT (Strengths, Weaknesses, Opportunities, Threats) analysis. Set a clear roadmap for achieving sales objectives.
- ✓ **Customer Relationship Management**: Sales managers oversee the management of customer relationships to ensure satisfaction and retention.
  Action Plan: Implement a Customer Relationship Management (CRM) system to track interactions, customer preferences, and feedback. Encourage the team to build lasting customer relationships.

Differentiating Sales Management from Sales Representation

The role of a sales manager differs significantly from that of a sales representative:

- ✓ **Sales Representatives**: Sales reps are primarily focused on selling products or services to customers. Their responsibilities include prospecting, pitching, and closing deals. They often have individual sales targets and are on the front lines of customer interactions.
- ✓ **Sales Managers**: Sales managers, on the other hand, are responsible for overseeing a team of sales representatives. Their role is more strategic and involves setting targets, coaching team members, and ensuring the team's collective success. While they may still engage in selling, their focus shifts towards managing and enabling their team to excel.

Example: Let's consider John, a successful sales representative who consistently meets his targets. His skills in prospecting and closing deals are exceptional. However, when promoted to a sales manager role, John faces a new set of responsibilities. He must now ensure not only his own success but also that of his team. This shift requires him to develop leadership, coaching, and strategic planning skills, which are distinct from the skills that made him a top sales rep.

A sales manager is the linchpin of a successful sales team, responsible for leadership, goal-setting, performance management, strategic planning, and customer relationship management. Understanding how this role differs from that of a sales representative is crucial for anyone aspiring to excel in sales management. In the following chapters, we will delve deeper into each of these responsibilities, providing practical guidance and strategies for success.

Why Develop Professionalism as a Sales Manager? Benefits & Repercussions

Developing professionalism as a Sales Manager is crucial for numerous reasons, and there are significant advantages and benefits associated with doing so. Failure to develop professionally can lead to several repercussions. Let's explore both sides of this issue:

Advantages and Benefits of Developing Professionalism:

- ✓ **Enhanced Credibility**: Sales Managers who display professionalism are more credible in the eyes of their teams, peers, and superiors. This credibility can positively influence team morale and trust.
- ✓ **Improved Leadership**: Professionalism fosters effective leadership. When Sales Managers lead by example, they inspire their teams to follow suit and perform at their best.
- ✓ **Better Customer Relationships**: Professionalism in interactions with clients builds trust and strengthens customer relationships, which can lead to increased sales and customer loyalty.
- ✓ **Higher Performance**: A professional Sales Manager is more likely to set high standards and encourage their team to meet and exceed targets, ultimately resulting in improved performance and productivity.
- ✓ **Effective Communication**: Professionalism promotes clear and respectful communication,

reducing misunderstandings and conflicts within the team and with customers.

- ✓ **Personal Growth**: Developing professionalism often involves personal growth and self-improvement. This can lead to increased job satisfaction and overall well-being.
- ✓ **Career Advancement**: Professionals tend to have more significant opportunities for career advancement. Developing professionalism can open doors to higher-level positions in sales management and beyond.
- ✓ **Positive Company Image**: A professional Sales Manager reflects positively on the company, attracting both clients and talented sales professionals.
- ✓ **Adaptability**: Professionalism often includes adaptability and a willingness to learn and grow, which is essential in an ever-changing business environment.

Repercussions of Not Developing Further:

- ✓ **Low Morale**: A lack of professionalism can lead to low team morale and decreased motivation, resulting in poor performance and high turnover rates.
- ✓ **Ineffective Leadership**: Unprofessional behavior can undermine a Sales Manager's authority and effectiveness as a leader, leading to a disorganized and underperforming team.
- ✓ **Lost Sales Opportunities**: Unprofessional conduct can drive away potential clients and harm existing customer relationships, resulting in lost sales opportunities and revenue.

- ✓ **Poor Reputation**: Sales Managers who don't develop professionally may earn a poor reputation within the industry, making it difficult to build relationships and secure partnerships.
- ✓ **Missed Career Growth**: Without professionalism, it's challenging to advance in one's career. Sales Managers may find themselves stuck in their current roles with limited prospects for growth.
- ✓ **Legal and Ethical Issues**: Unprofessional behavior can lead to legal and ethical problems, including compliance violations, which can result in fines and damage to the company's reputation.
- ✓ **Internal Conflicts**: Unprofessionalism often leads to conflicts within the team, hindering collaboration and cohesion.
- ✓ **Customer Loss**: Unprofessional interactions with clients can result in customer loss and damage the company's brand image.
- ✓ **Stagnation**: Without a commitment to professionalism and personal growth, Sales Managers may become stagnant in their knowledge and skills, unable to adapt to changing market conditions.

The advantages and benefits of developing professionalism as a Sales Manager are numerous and extend to both personal and organizational levels. On the other hand, the repercussions of not developing further can have a detrimental impact on team performance, customer relationships, and career progression. Therefore, it is essential for Sales Managers to continually invest in their professional development to thrive in their roles and contribute positively to their organizations.

Understanding the Key Responsibilities of Sales Managers

Sales Managers play a crucial role in driving revenue and achieving organizational goals. Here are key responsibilities of Sales Managers along with examples and action plans on how to develop them:

1. Leadership and Team Building:

Responsibility: Provide strong leadership to the sales team, build a cohesive and motivated team, and foster a positive work culture.

Example: Lead by example, set clear expectations, and inspire your team to achieve their targets.

Action Plan:

- ✓ Conduct leadership training to enhance your leadership skills.
- ✓ Regularly communicate the company's vision and values to inspire your team.
- ✓ Encourage collaboration and teamwork through team-building activities.

2. Goal Setting and Planning:

Responsibility: Define clear sales objectives, create sales plans, and develop strategies to achieve targets.

Example: Set SMART (Specific, Measurable, Achievable, Relevant, Time-bound) goals for each sales representative.

Action Plan:

- ✓ Learn about goal-setting techniques and apply them in your planning.
- ✓ Collaborate with your team to create sales plans and set realistic targets.

- ✓ Regularly review and adjust your sales plans based on performance data.

3. Sales Training and Development:

Responsibility: Develop and deliver effective sales training programs, ensuring that your team is well-equipped with the necessary skills and knowledge.

Example: Provide product knowledge training to your team to enhance their ability to explain product features to customers.

Action Plan:

- ✓ Identify training needs through performance evaluations.
- ✓ Invest in sales training resources and external courses.
- ✓ Monitor the effectiveness of training programs and adjust them as needed.

4. Performance Management:

Responsibility: Monitor and evaluate individual and team performance, provide feedback, and take corrective actions when necessary.

Example: Regularly review sales reports to assess the performance of each sales representative.

Action Plan:

- ✓ Develop performance evaluation criteria and KPIs for your team.
- ✓ Conduct regular performance reviews and set improvement goals.
- ✓ Provide coaching and support to help team members meet their targets.

5. Sales Strategy and Planning:

Responsibility: Develop and implement sales strategies that align with the company's goals and market conditions.

Example: Create a strategic plan for expanding into a new market segment.

Action Plan:

- ✓ Stay updated on industry trends and competitive intelligence.
- ✓ Collaborate with other departments to align sales strategies with marketing and product development efforts.
- ✓ Continuously evaluate and adjust your sales strategies based on market dynamics.

6. Customer Relationship Management:

Responsibility: Build and maintain strong relationships with key customers and stakeholders.

Example: Schedule regular meetings with key clients to understand their needs and address any issues.

Action Plan:

- ✓ Develop a customer relationship management strategy.
- ✓ Train your team on effective communication and relationship-building techniques.
- ✓ Implement CRM software to streamline customer interactions and data management.

7. Sales Forecasting and Budgeting:

Responsibility: Forecast sales revenues, allocate budgets, and manage resources effectively.

Example: Develop a sales forecast for the next quarter based on historical data and market trends.

Action Plan:

- ✓ Learn about sales forecasting models and techniques.
- ✓ Collaborate with finance to allocate budgets based on sales forecasts.
- ✓ Regularly review and adjust budgets as needed to optimize resource allocation.

8. Data Analytics and Decision-Making:

Responsibility: Use data analytics to make informed decisions, track performance, and identify areas for improvement.
Example: Analyze customer data to identify patterns and preferences.
Action Plan:

- ✓ Develop data analysis skills or hire a data analyst for your team.
- ✓ Implement data analytics tools to track KPIs and gather actionable insights.
- ✓ Use data-driven insights to make strategic decisions.

9. Conflict Resolution and Problem Solving:
Responsibility: Address conflicts within the sales team and solve problems that hinder sales performance.
Example: Mediate conflicts between team members and find resolutions that improve team dynamics.
Action Plan:

- ✓ Learn conflict resolution techniques and communication skills.
- ✓ Establish a conflict resolution process within your team.
- ✓ Encourage open communication to address issues as they arise.

10. Communication and Reporting:
Responsibility: Ensure clear and effective communication within the sales team and provide regular reports to senior management.
Example: Hold weekly team meetings to discuss goals, challenges, and strategies.
Action Plan:

- ✓ Improve your communication skills, both verbal and written.

- ✓ Establish a reporting schedule and format to keep senior management informed.
- ✓ Encourage transparent communication within your team to foster collaboration.

By developing these key responsibilities and consistently applying them, you can become an effective and successful Sales Manager, driving your team towards achieving outstanding results. Continuous learning, self-improvement, and adaptability are essential to excel in this role.

Key Characteristics/ Traits and Attributes of Effective Sales Managers

Key characteristics, traits, and attributes of effective Sales Managers are vital for success in this role. Here's a list with examples and action plans on how to develop them:

1. Leadership:

Characteristic: Sales Managers need to lead and inspire their sales teams to achieve goals.

Example: Lead by setting a strong example, motivating the team, and making tough decisions when necessary.

Action Plan:

- ✓ Seek leadership training or coaching to develop leadership skills.
- ✓ Identify role models in leadership and learn from their experiences.
- ✓ Regularly communicate the company's vision to inspire your team.

2. Communication Skills:

Characteristic: Effective communication is essential for conveying expectations, providing feedback, and building relationships.

Example: Clearly articulate sales targets and provide constructive feedback to team members.

Action Plan:

- ✓ Take communication courses or workshops to improve your skills.
- ✓ Practice active listening to better understand your team's needs.

- ✓ Foster open and transparent communication within your team.

3. Adaptability:

Characteristic: Sales Managers must adapt to changing market conditions, customer preferences, and organizational goals.

Example: Adjust sales strategies in response to shifts in the market or industry trends.

Action Plan:

- ✓ Embrace change and stay updated on industry trends and best practices.
- ✓ Encourage a culture of adaptability within your team.
- ✓ Be open to feedback and be willing to adjust your approach when needed.

4. Strategic Thinking:

Characteristic: Sales Managers need to think strategically to set goals and develop plans for achieving them.

Example: Develop long-term sales strategies that align with the company's objectives.

Action Plan:

- ✓ Study strategic thinking models and frameworks.
- ✓ Collaborate with other departments to align sales strategies with overall business goals.
- ✓ Regularly assess and adjust your sales strategies to stay on course.

5. Empathy:

Characteristic: Understanding and relating to your team's challenges and concerns is crucial for effective leadership.

Example: Show empathy by actively listening to your team members and providing support when they face difficulties.

Action Plan:

- ✓ Practice empathy by putting yourself in your team's shoes.
- ✓ Hold regular one-on-one meetings to discuss team members' concerns and offer assistance.
- ✓ Develop a culture of support and collaboration within your team.

6. Decision-Making Skills:

Characteristic: Sales Managers often need to make tough decisions quickly.

Example: Make informed decisions on sales strategies, resource allocation, and personnel management.

Action Plan:

- ✓ Enhance your decision-making skills through training and by seeking mentorship.
- ✓ Develop a structured decision-making process that includes data analysis and consultation when needed.
- ✓ Review and analyze past decisions to learn and improve.

7. Accountability:

Characteristic: Taking ownership of results and being accountable for both successes and failures is crucial.

Example: Accept responsibility for team performance and take corrective actions when necessary.

Action Plan:

- ✓ Create a culture of accountability within your team by setting clear expectations.
- ✓ Hold yourself and your team members accountable for meeting targets and goals.

- ✓ Conduct regular performance reviews to assess progress and identify areas for improvement.

8. Time Management:

Characteristic: Sales Managers must effectively prioritize tasks and manage their time to meet objectives.

Example: Allocate time for strategic planning, team meetings, and individual coaching sessions.

Action Plan:

- ✓ Implement time management techniques like the Eisenhower Matrix or the Pomodoro Technique.
- ✓ Use digital tools and calendars to schedule tasks and reminders.
- ✓ Delegate tasks when appropriate to free up time for critical responsibilities.

9. Resilience:

Characteristic: Sales Managers need to stay resilient in the face of rejection and setbacks.

Example: Bounce back from losing a major client by quickly reevaluating and adjusting sales strategies.

Action Plan:

- ✓ Develop a growth mindset that views setbacks as opportunities to learn and improve.
- ✓ Encourage your team to embrace resilience as well by sharing stories of overcoming challenges.
- ✓ Seek support from mentors or peers to help build your resilience.

10. Conflict Resolution Skills:

Characteristic: Conflict may arise within the team or with clients, and Sales Managers need to handle these situations effectively.

Example: Resolve disputes between team members or address issues with dissatisfied customers.
Action Plan:

- ✓ Learn conflict resolution techniques and practice them regularly.
- ✓ Establish a clear conflict resolution process within your team.
- ✓ Promote open communication to address issues as they arise and prevent escalation.

Developing these characteristics and attributes requires ongoing effort and self-improvement. Consider enrolling in relevant courses, seeking mentorship, and continuously seeking feedback from your team and colleagues to refine and strengthen these traits as you progress in your role as a Sales Manager.

Recruiting and On-boarding

Recruiting top talent and ensuring they integrate seamlessly into your sales team is a critical function of a sales manager. This chapter explores strategies for effective recruiting and on-boarding processes to maximize the potential of new team members.

Strategies for Effective Recruiting

Recruiting the right individuals can make or break a sales team. Here are some strategies to ensure you're bringing in top-notch talent:

- ✓ **Define the Ideal Candidate**: Start by clearly defining what you're looking for in a salesperson. Consider factors like experience, skills, and cultural fit with your team and organization.
  Action Plan: Create a detailed job description and person specification that outlines the qualifications and qualities you're seeking.
- ✓ **Leverage Multiple Channels**: Use a variety of recruitment channels, including job boards, social media, employee referrals, and professional networks, to reach a diverse pool of candidates.
  Action Plan: Develop a recruitment marketing plan that outlines where and how you'll advertise job openings.
- ✓ **Structured Interview Process**: Establish a structured interview process that includes behavioral and situational questions to assess a candidate's skills and fit for the role.
  Action Plan: Create interview scripts and evaluation rubrics to standardize the interview process.

- ✓ **Assessment Tests**: Consider using assessment tests or simulations to gauge a candidate's sales aptitude and skills.
  Action Plan: Identify or develop appropriate sales assessment tools and integrate them into your hiring process.
- ✓ **Check References**: Conduct thorough reference checks to verify a candidate's background and qualifications.
  Action Plan: Develop a reference check questionnaire and ensure all references are contacted.

On-boarding Processes to Ensure Seamless Integration

Once you've recruited promising candidates, the next crucial step is on-boarding to ensure they integrate seamlessly into your sales team. Effective on-boarding contributes to faster productivity and long-term employee satisfaction.

- ✓ **Preparation**: Before the new team member's first day, prepare their workspace, equipment, and access to necessary tools and systems.
  Action Plan: Create a checklist for IT setup, workspace preparation, and provisioning of necessary materials.
- ✓ **Orientation**: Provide an orientation session that covers the company's culture, mission, values, and an overview of the sales team's goals and objectives.
  Action Plan: Develop an orientation agenda and welcome packet.
- ✓ **Training**: Implement a structured training program that includes product knowledge, sales techniques, and the use of sales tools and software.

Action Plan: Develop a training schedule with clear learning objectives and milestones.

- ✓ **Mentorship**: Assign a mentor or buddy to help new team members acclimate to the team, answer questions, and provide guidance.
  Action Plan: Identify potential mentors within your team and establish a mentorship program.
- ✓ **Regular Check-ins**: Conduct regular check-in meetings during the initial weeks to address any concerns or questions and provide feedback.
  Action Plan: Schedule weekly check-ins for the first month and bi-weekly for the following two months.
- ✓ **Performance Expectations**: Clearly communicate performance expectations, KPIs, and milestones for the new team member's probation period.
  Action Plan: Develop a performance plan that outlines targets and expectations.

Example: Imagine you've just hired Sarah, a sales representative with great potential. To ensure her seamless integration into the team, you've provided her with a detailed on-boarding schedule that includes orientation, product training, and regular check-ins with her assigned mentor, Alex. Sarah not only quickly becomes productive but also feels supported and engaged from day one.

Effective recruiting and on-boarding are essential for building a high-performing sales team. By following these strategies and action plans, you can attract top talent and ensure that they become valuable assets to your organization. In the following chapters, we will explore more aspects of sales management to help you drive exceptional results through your team.

Team Building and Leadership

Building a cohesive and high-performing sales team is a fundamental task for a sales manager. In this chapter, we'll explore techniques for creating a strong team and examine various leadership styles and their impact on team dynamics.

Techniques for Building a Cohesive Sales Team

- ✓ **Define a Clear Vision**: Start by defining a compelling vision for your sales team. This vision should provide a sense of purpose and direction, motivating team members to work together toward common goals.
  Action Plan: Create a vision statement that articulates the team's mission and values. Communicate this vision regularly.
- ✓ **Hiring the Right People**: Building a cohesive team starts with recruiting individuals who not only have the necessary skills but also fit well within the team's culture.
  Action Plan: Implement a hiring process that assesses both technical skills and cultural fit.
- ✓ **Effective Communication**: Establish open and transparent communication channels within the team. Encourage team members to share ideas, feedback, and concerns.
  Action Plan: Schedule regular team meetings, one-on-one discussions, and create a digital platform for easy communication.
- ✓ **Team-Building Activities**: Organize team-building activities and exercises to foster trust and collaboration among team members.

Action Plan: Plan quarterly team-building events or workshops that encourage cooperation and build camaraderie.

- ✓ **Setting Clear Roles and Responsibilities**: Ensure that every team member understands their role and responsibilities. This reduces confusion and minimizes conflicts.
  Action Plan: Develop clear job descriptions and role expectations for each team member.
- ✓ **Promote a Growth Mindset**: Encourage a growth mindset within the team, where members believe in their ability to improve and learn from both successes and failures.
  Action Plan: Provide opportunities for skill development and offer constructive feedback to promote growth.

Leadership Styles and Their Impact on Team Dynamics

Different leadership styles can have a profound impact on team dynamics. Here are some leadership styles and their implications:

- ✓ **Transformational Leadership**: Transformational leaders inspire and motivate their teams by setting high expectations and providing support.
  Action Plan: If you adopt a transformational leadership style, regularly communicate your vision, inspire innovation, and offer mentorship to your team.
- ✓ **Transactional Leadership**: Transactional leaders focus on goals and performance metrics. They use rewards and punishments to motivate their teams.
  Action Plan: If you lean towards transactional leadership, clearly define expectations,

provide regular performance feedback, and implement a rewards system for achieving targets.

- ✓ **Servant Leadership**: Servant leaders prioritize the needs of their team members and work to support their growth and development.
  Action Plan: To embrace servant leadership, actively listen to your team, provide resources for their success, and prioritize their well-being.
- ✓ **Democratic Leadership**: Democratic leaders involve the team in decision-making, fostering a sense of ownership and responsibility.
  Action Plan: If you prefer a democratic leadership style, solicit input from team members when making decisions and consider their ideas seriously.
- ✓ **Autocratic Leadership**: Autocratic leaders make decisions unilaterally, with little input from the team.
  Action Plan: If you lean towards an autocratic style, ensure that your team understands your decision-making process and the rationale behind your choices.

Example: Consider a sales manager, Mike, who adopts a transformational leadership style. He communicates a compelling vision for the team's success and encourages innovation. Mike consistently supports his team members' development, offering coaching and mentorship. As a result, his sales team not only meets their targets but consistently exceeds them, driven by their shared commitment to the team's vision.

In conclusion, building a cohesive sales team involves setting a clear vision, hiring the right people, fostering open communication, and defining roles and responsibilities. Leadership style plays a significant role in team dynamics, so it's essential to choose a style that aligns with your team's needs and your personal strengths. By implementing the action plans and strategies outlined in this chapter, you can create a high-performing sales team that excels under your leadership.

Setting Goals and Sales Targets

Setting clear and effective goals is a fundamental aspect of sales management. In this chapter, we'll explore how to set SMART (Specific, Measurable, Achievable, Relevant, Time-bound) goals and establish sales targets and quotas to drive your sales team's performance.

How to Set SMART Goals

SMART goals are designed to provide clarity, structure, and focus. Here's how to create them:

- ✓ **Specific:** Your goal should be well-defined and clear. It should answer the questions of "what," "why," and "how."

  Action Plan: Instead of a vague goal like "Increase sales," specify it as "Increase sales of Product A by 15% in the next quarter by targeting the healthcare sector."
- ✓ **Measurable:** Your goal should include criteria that allow you to track progress and determine when you've achieved it.

  Action Plan: Use concrete metrics like revenue, units sold, or customer acquisitions to measure your progress.
- ✓ **Achievable:** Ensure that your goal is realistic and attainable given your team's resources and capabilities.

  Action Plan: Consider whether the goal is within your team's reach, given current market conditions and available resources.
- ✓ **Relevant:** The goal should align with your team's broader objectives and the organization's mission.

Action Plan: Assess whether achieving the goal will contribute to the team's overall success and the organization's strategic goals.

- ✓ **Time-bound:** Set a specific timeframe for achieving the goal. This creates a sense of urgency and accountability.
  Action Plan: Specify a deadline, such as "Increase monthly sales by 10% within the next three months."

Establishing Sales Targets and Quotas

Sales targets and quotas provide concrete benchmarks that guide your team's efforts. Here's how to establish them effectively:

- ✓ **Analyze Historical Data:** Start by reviewing past sales performance data to identify trends, seasonality, and growth patterns.
  Action Plan: Collect historical sales data, segment it by product, region, or salesperson, and identify areas for improvement.
- ✓ **Consider Market Conditions:** Take into account the current market conditions, industry trends, and competitive landscape when setting targets.
  Action Plan: Stay updated on market news, conduct competitor analysis, and adjust targets accordingly.
- ✓ **Assess Team Capacity:** Evaluate your team's capabilities, including their skills, experience, and workload, to determine realistic quotas.
  Action Plan: Conduct performance reviews and skill assessments to identify areas where additional training or resources are needed.

- ✓ **Collaborative Goal-Setting:** Involve your sales team in the goal-setting process to ensure buy-in and motivation.
  Action Plan: Hold team meetings to discuss and agree upon targets, allowing team members to provide input and insights.
- ✓ **Break Down Targets:** Divide larger targets into smaller, more manageable goals for individual team members. Ensure these individual targets contribute to the overall team goal.
  Action Plan: Assign specific targets to each team member based on their role and capabilities.

Example: Imagine you're a sales manager for a software company. You've decided to launch a new product and want to set SMART goals and sales targets for your team. After conducting market research, you decide on the following:

- ✓ Specific: "Increase sales of our new software product by 20% in the next six months by targeting the finance and healthcare sectors."
- ✓ Measurable: Measure progress through monthly sales reports and tracking the number of new clients acquired.
- ✓ Achievable: Based on market demand and your team's capabilities, a 20% increase seems achievable.
- ✓ Relevant: Increasing sales of the new product aligns with your organization's strategic goal of expanding market share.
- ✓ Time-bound: The goal is set for the next six months.
- ✓ For sales targets and quotas, you break down the overall target by assigning specific sales

goals to each team member based on their experience and strengths. The targets are designed to collectively achieve the 20% increase.

In conclusion, setting SMART goals and establishing sales targets and quotas are essential for guiding your sales team's efforts and measuring their progress. By following the action plans and strategies outlined in this chapter, you can ensure that your goals are well-defined, achievable, and aligned with your team's capabilities and your organization's objectives.

Sales Training and Development

Sales training and continuous skill development are essential for maintaining a competitive and high-performing sales team. In this chapter, we'll explore how to design a comprehensive sales training program and implement ongoing learning strategies.

Designing a Comprehensive Sales Training Program

A well-structured sales training program can equip your team with the skills and knowledge they need to excel. Here's how to design one effectively:

- ✓ **Assess Training Needs**: Start by conducting a thorough assessment of your team's training needs. Identify gaps in skills, knowledge, and competencies.
  Action Plan: Conduct skills assessments, review performance metrics, and gather feedback from team members.
- ✓ **Define Training Objectives**: Clearly outline the specific learning objectives you want to achieve through the training program.
  Action Plan: Develop a list of specific skills or knowledge areas that the program will address, such as objection handling, product knowledge, or negotiation skills.
- ✓ **Create Curriculum and Content**: Develop a curriculum that covers all necessary topics and modules. Create engaging content, including presentations, videos, role-playing exercises, and quizzes.
  Action Plan: Collaborate with subject matter experts or trainers to create content that is engaging and interactive.

- ✓ **Choose Training Methods**: Select appropriate training methods based on your team's learning preferences and needs. This can include classroom training, online courses, workshops, or on-the-job training.
  Action Plan: Mix different training methods to accommodate various learning styles. For example, use e-learning modules for self-paced learning and conduct in-person workshops for hands-on practice.
- ✓ **Schedule Training Sessions**: Plan and schedule training sessions, taking into account the team's workload and availability.
  Action Plan: Create a training calendar that outlines when and where each training session will take place.
- ✓ **Measure Training Effectiveness**: Implement assessments and evaluations to measure the effectiveness of the training program.
  Action Plan: Develop pre- and post-training assessments to gauge knowledge gain. Collect feedback from participants to identify areas for improvement.
- ✓ **Continuous Improvement**: Continuously review and update the training program to keep it current and relevant.
  Action Plan: Conduct regular reviews of training materials and adjust them based on feedback and changes in the industry.

Continuous Learning and Skill Development for Sales Teams

Sales professionals must engage in continuous learning to stay competitive. Here's how to foster a culture of ongoing skill development:

- ✓ **Encourage Self-Directed Learning**: Encourage team members to take ownership of their learning by seeking out resources and training opportunities.
  Action Plan: Provide access to a library of sales resources, books, and online courses. Encourage team members to set aside time for self-study.
- ✓ **Offer Coaching and Mentorship**: Assign mentors or coaches within the team to provide guidance, share experiences, and offer constructive feedback.
  Action Plan: Pair experienced team members with newcomers for mentorship. Schedule regular coaching sessions to review performance and set development goals.
- ✓ **Promote Cross-Training**: Encourage team members to learn from each other by sharing best practices and experiences.
  Action Plan: Organize regular knowledge-sharing sessions or peer-to-peer training workshops.
- ✓ **Support Certifications and Professional Development**: Provide support for team members to pursue industry certifications and attend relevant conferences and seminars.
  Action Plan: Offer financial incentives or paid time off for team members who complete certifications or attend industry events.
- ✓ **Performance-Based Training**: Tailor training and development opportunities to individual performance goals and improvement areas.
  Action Plan: During performance reviews, identify specific training needs and create customized development plans.

Example: Let's say you're a sales manager at a tech company, and your team is transitioning to selling a new software product. You assess that your team lacks in-depth knowledge of the product. To address this, you design a comprehensive training program that includes online courses, hands-on workshops, and role-playing exercises. You also bring in product experts to conduct training sessions.

To promote continuous learning, you encourage your team to take advantage of the company's subscription to industry-specific e-learning platforms. You assign mentors to newer team members and create a certification program that rewards team members for completing product knowledge courses. As a result, your team becomes well-versed in the new product, leading to increased confidence and better sales performance.

In conclusion, a comprehensive sales training program and a culture of continuous learning are crucial for keeping your sales team competitive and adaptable. By following the action plans and strategies outlined in this chapter, you can ensure that your team is equipped with the skills and knowledge needed to excel in a dynamic sales environment.

Motivation and Incentive Programs

Motivating your sales team is vital for boosting morale and performance. In this chapter, we'll explore incentive structures and motivation techniques that can drive your sales professionals to excel.

Incentive Structures to Boost Team Morale and Performance

- ✓ **Commission-Based Compensation**: Offering commissions for sales is a classic incentive structure. It directly ties earnings to performance and can be highly motivating.
  Action Plan: Define clear commission structures that reward higher sales volumes or larger deals. Consider tiered commission rates to incentivize top performers even more.
- ✓ **Performance Bonuses**: Performance-based bonuses are one-time rewards for achieving specific targets. They can provide a significant motivational boost.
  Action Plan: Set clear bonus criteria and communicate them to the team. Consider offering bonuses for surpassing quarterly or annual sales targets.
- ✓ **Sales Contests and Competitions**: Organize sales contests with enticing prizes to spark healthy competition and drive results.
  Action Plan: Plan contests around specific sales objectives or product launches. Ensure that the prizes are attractive and meaningful to your team.

- ✓ **Recognition and Awards**: Recognizing top performers publicly within the team or company can boost morale and motivation.
  Action Plan: Create a "Salesperson of the Month" or "Top Sales Team" award. Hold regular recognition events or ceremonies.
- ✓ **Profit Sharing**: Some organizations offer profit-sharing programs where a portion of the company's profits is distributed among employees.
  Action Plan: Establish a profit-sharing policy and communicate how it works. Ensure that the sharing aligns with sales team performance.

Motivation Techniques for Sales Professionals

- ✓ **Goal Setting**: Encourage your team members to set clear, achievable goals for themselves. This gives them a sense of direction and purpose.
  Action Plan: Help each team member define their individual sales goals and assist them in breaking these goals into smaller, manageable steps.
- ✓ **Positive Reinforcement**: Use positive reinforcement to reward desired behaviors. Recognize and celebrate achievements, no matter how small.
  Action Plan: Offer immediate verbal praise or written recognition when a salesperson meets a milestone or exhibits exemplary behavior.
- ✓ **Career Development**: Motivate your team by showing them a clear career path within the organization. Offer opportunities for growth and advancement.

Action Plan: Discuss potential career paths with team members during performance reviews. Identify skill gaps and recommend training or coaching to help them progress.

- ✓ **Feedback and Coaching**: Regularly provide constructive feedback and coaching to help your team improve. Constructive feedback demonstrates that you care about their success.

  Action Plan: Schedule regular one-on-one coaching sessions with team members. Use a "sandwich" approach, where you start and end with positive feedback and insert constructive feedback in the middle.

- ✓ **Flexible Work Environment**: Offer flexibility when possible, such as remote work options or flexible hours. This can boost job satisfaction and motivation.

  Action Plan: Develop a flexible work policy that outlines guidelines and expectations for remote work or flexible hours.

Example: Let's say you're the sales manager at a telecommunications company, and you want to boost motivation and performance among your sales team. You decide to implement a quarterly sales contest called the "Top Performer Challenge." The winner of each quarter receives an all-expenses-paid weekend getaway for themselves and a guest.

To keep motivation high throughout the year, you set up monthly recognition awards for the "Rising Star" and "Customer Champion." These awards come with cash bonuses and public recognition during team meetings.

Additionally, you provide individualized coaching sessions to each team member, focusing on their strengths and areas for improvement. This personalized approach helps boost their confidence and motivation to excel.

In conclusion, effective motivation and incentive programs can significantly impact your sales team's performance and morale. By implementing the action plans and strategies outlined in this chapter, you can create a work environment that inspires your sales professionals to achieve their best and drive outstanding results.

Sales Planning and Strategy

Effective sales planning and strategy are vital for achieving organizational objectives. In this chapter, we'll delve into the process of developing a sales plan aligned with broader goals and explore the importance of strategic thinking in sales management.

Developing a Sales Plan Aligned with Organizational Objectives

- ✓ **Understand Organizational Goals**: Start by gaining a deep understanding of your organization's broader goals and objectives. What is the company trying to achieve in the short term and long term?
  Action Plan: Schedule meetings with senior leadership and department heads to align your sales plan with the overarching organizational strategy.
- ✓ **Market Analysis**: Conduct a comprehensive analysis of your target market. Who are your ideal customers? What are their needs, pain points, and preferences?
  Action Plan: Invest in market research to gather data on customer demographics, market trends, and competitive landscape.
- ✓ **Set Clear Sales Objectives**: Define specific sales objectives that align with the organizational goals. These objectives should be SMART (Specific, Measurable, Achievable, Relevant, Time-bound).
  Action Plan: Break down the broader organizational goals into smaller, department-specific targets. For example, if the company

aims to increase market share by 10%, your sales objective might be to acquire 15% more customers in your target market.

- ✓ **Resource Allocation**: Determine the resources required to achieve your sales objectives. This includes budget, personnel, technology, and tools.
  Action Plan: Create a detailed resource allocation plan, specifying how budget and personnel will be distributed across various sales initiatives.
- ✓ **Sales Strategies**: Develop strategies to achieve your sales objectives. Consider pricing strategies, distribution channels, product positioning, and marketing efforts.
  Action Plan: Collaborate with your marketing team to align messaging and promotional activities with your sales strategies.
- ✓ **Sales Tactics and Action Plans**: Outline specific tactics and action plans to implement your strategies. These are the day-to-day activities your sales team will engage in.
  Action Plan: Create a detailed sales playbook that includes scripts, templates, and step-by-step guides for various sales scenarios.
- ✓ **Performance Metrics**: Define key performance indicators (KPIs) that will help you track progress toward your sales objectives.
  Action Plan: Implement a performance measurement system that provides real-time data on sales team performance and pipeline progress.

Strategic Thinking in Sales Management

- ✓ **Long-Term Vision**: Encourage your sales team to think beyond immediate targets and focus on the long-term vision. How can your sales efforts contribute to the company's future growth?
  Action Plan: Schedule regular strategy sessions with your team to discuss long-term goals and strategies.
- ✓ **Competitive Analysis**: Continuously monitor the competitive landscape. What are your competitors doing, and how can you differentiate your offerings?
  Action Plan: Set up automated tools or services to track competitor activities and gather insights.
- ✓ **Customer-Centric Approach**: Place the customer at the center of your strategy. How can you meet their evolving needs and expectations?
  Action Plan: Conduct customer surveys and feedback sessions to gather insights into their preferences and pain points.
- ✓ **Adaptability**: Be open to adapting your strategies and tactics based on changing market conditions and customer feedback.
  Action Plan: Create a culture of adaptability within your team by encouraging feedback and innovation.
- ✓ **Risk Management**: Identify potential risks and challenges that could impact your sales efforts and develop contingency plans.
  Action Plan: Conduct a SWOT analysis (Strengths, Weaknesses, Opportunities, Threats) to identify potential risks and opportunities.

Example: Imagine you're the sales manager for a software company aiming to increase its market share in the education technology sector. To align your sales plan with organizational objectives, you start by meeting with the CEO and the head of product development to understand the company's long-term vision. They want to expand into emerging markets and become a leader in educational software within five years.

You conduct thorough market research, identifying key growth opportunities and potential customer segments. Based on this research, you set clear sales objectives, such as acquiring 20% more customers in emerging markets within the next year.

Your sales strategies include competitive pricing, partnerships with educational institutions, and targeted marketing campaigns. You outline specific sales tactics, such as conducting product demos and providing educational resources to customers.

To foster strategic thinking, you organize regular strategy sessions with your sales team. During these sessions, you discuss the evolving needs of educational institutions and brainstorm ways to adapt the product to meet those needs.

In conclusion, developing a sales plan aligned with organizational objectives and fostering strategic thinking are critical for sales management success. By implementing the action plans and strategies outlined in this chapter, you can create a roadmap that guides your sales team toward achieving both short-term targets and long-term growth objectives.

Performance Management

Performance management is crucial for maintaining and improving the effectiveness of your sales team. In this chapter, we'll explore methods for assessing individual and team performance, as well as providing constructive feedback and coaching.

Methods for Assessing Individual and Team Performance

- ✓ **Key Performance Indicators (KPIs)**: Identify and track KPIs that align with your sales objectives. Common KPIs include sales revenue, conversion rates, customer acquisition costs, and customer retention rates.
  Action Plan: Define specific KPIs for each sales role and regularly update dashboards or reports to monitor performance against these metrics.
- ✓ **Sales Metrics**: In addition to KPIs, measure other relevant sales metrics, such as lead response time, sales cycle length, and win-loss ratios.
  Action Plan: Utilize sales analytics tools to gather and analyze data on these metrics. Share insights with the team to drive improvement.
- ✓ **Sales Quotas**: Set individual and team sales quotas based on historical data, market analysis, and organizational objectives.
  Action Plan: Discuss quotas with team members to ensure they are challenging yet attainable. Monitor progress toward quotas throughout the year.

- ✓ **Customer Feedback**: Collect and analyze customer feedback to assess the quality of interactions and overall satisfaction with the sales team.
  Action Plan: Implement post-sale surveys and conduct regular account reviews to gather customer insights.
- ✓ **Competitive Benchmarking**: Compare your team's performance against industry benchmarks and competitors to identify areas for improvement.
  Action Plan: Invest in market research and industry reports to gain insights into how your team stacks up against the competition.

Providing Constructive Feedback and Coaching

- ✓ **Regular Performance Reviews**: Conduct regular performance reviews with team members to discuss their progress, achievements, and areas for improvement.
  Action Plan: Schedule quarterly or bi-annual performance reviews to provide a structured platform for feedback and goal setting.
- ✓ **Specific and Actionable Feedback**: Provide feedback that is specific, actionable, and focused on behavior or results.
  Action Plan: Use the Situation-Behavior-Impact (SBI) framework to structure feedback. Describe the situation, the observed behavior, and the impact it had.
- ✓ **Strengths-Based Approach**: Recognize and leverage each team member's strengths. Encourage them to use their strengths to excel in their roles.

Action Plan: During coaching sessions, discuss individual strengths and how they can be applied to achieve sales goals.

✓ **Goal Setting**: Collaboratively set performance goals and development objectives with each team member. Ensure that these goals align with both individual growth and organizational targets.

Action Plan: Use the SMART (Specific, Measurable, Achievable, Relevant, Time-bound) framework to define clear and actionable goals.

✓ **Coaching and Skill Development**: Provide ongoing coaching and skill development opportunities. Offer resources, training, and mentorship to help team members improve.

Action Plan: Schedule regular coaching sessions to discuss progress and areas for development. Encourage team members to attend relevant training programs or courses.

Example: Let's say you manage a sales team for a software company. To assess individual and team performance, you regularly review sales dashboards that track KPIs such as monthly revenue, lead conversion rates, and customer churn.

During performance reviews, you use the SBI framework to provide feedback to each team member. For instance, you might say, "In the recent sales call with Client X (situation), I noticed that you effectively addressed their concerns and objections (behavior), which resulted in a successful contract renewal and positive feedback (impact)."

You collaborate with team members to set specific goals for the upcoming quarter, such as increasing monthly revenue by 15% or improving lead follow-up times. You provide coaching and mentorship to help them develop the skills needed to achieve these goals.

In conclusion, effective performance management is essential for optimizing your sales team's effectiveness and achieving organizational objectives. By implementing the action plans and strategies outlined in this chapter, you can create a culture of continuous improvement and ensure that your team members receive the support and feedback they need to excel in their roles.

Sales Metrics and Analytics

Sales metrics and analytics are essential tools for sales managers to measure performance, make informed decisions, and drive improvements. In this chapter, we'll explore key performance indicators (KPIs) for sales managers and how to use data analytics to enhance sales decision-making.

Key Performance Indicators (KPIs) for Sales Managers

- ✓ **Sales Revenue**: Sales revenue is a fundamental KPI that indicates how much revenue your sales team generates within a specific period.
  Action Plan: Track and analyze sales revenue by product, region, salesperson, and customer segment to identify areas for growth.
- ✓ **Customer Acquisition Cost (CAC)**: CAC measures the cost of acquiring a new customer. It's calculated by dividing your total sales and marketing expenses by the number of new customers acquired.
  Action Plan: Monitor CAC to ensure that your customer acquisition efforts are cost-effective. Identify strategies to reduce CAC while increasing customer acquisition.
- ✓ **Customer Lifetime Value (CLV)**: CLV represents the total revenue a customer is expected to generate throughout their relationship with your company.
  Action Plan: Focus on increasing CLV by providing exceptional customer service, up-selling, and retaining customers for longer periods.

- ✓ **Conversion Rate**: The conversion rate measures the percentage of leads that become paying customers.
  Action Plan: Analyze conversion rates at different stages of the sales funnel to pinpoint bottlenecks and optimize the sales process.
- ✓ **Sales Pipeline Value**: The total value of opportunities in your sales pipeline gives you an overview of potential revenue.
  Action Plan: Monitor the pipeline value and ensure that it aligns with your revenue targets. Identify strategies to move opportunities through the pipeline efficiently.
- ✓ **Lead Response Time**: The time it takes for your sales team to respond to leads can impact conversion rates.
  Action Plan: Implement processes and tools to reduce lead response time, such as automated lead assignment and response templates.

How to Use Data Analytics to Drive Sales Decisions

- ✓ **Data Collection**: Start by collecting relevant data from various sources, including CRM systems, marketing analytics tools, and customer feedback.
- ✓ *Action Plan*: Ensure that your team is accurately and consistently recording data in your systems.
- ✓ **Data Visualization**: Use data visualization tools and dashboards to transform raw data into actionable insights.
- ✓ *Action Plan*: Invest in data visualization software or work with data analysts to create custom dashboards.

- ✓ **Identify Trends**: Analyze historical data to identify trends and patterns in customer behavior, sales performance, and market dynamics.
- ✓ *Action Plan*: Regularly review historical data and conduct trend analysis to stay ahead of market changes.
- ✓ **Predictive Analytics**: Implement predictive analytics models to forecast future sales trends and customer behaviors.
- ✓ *Action Plan*: Collaborate with data scientists or use predictive analytics software to create models that predict sales outcomes.
- ✓ **Segmentation**: Segment your customer base based on demographics, behavior, or purchasing history to tailor marketing and sales strategies.
- ✓ *Action Plan*: Use customer segmentation to personalize marketing messages and product recommendations.

Example: Consider you're a sales manager for a software company. You notice a decline in sales revenue over the past quarter. To address this issue, you decide to use data analytics:

- ✓ **Data Collection**: You gather data from your CRM system, marketing automation tools, and customer surveys. You also collect information on leads, conversion rates, and customer feedback.
- ✓ **Data Visualization**: You create a dashboard that displays key metrics, including sales revenue, conversion rates, lead response times, and customer satisfaction scores. The dashboard updates in real-time.

- ✓ **Identify Trends**: After analyzing historical data, you notice that conversion rates drop significantly during the lead qualification stage. You also see that customers who receive personalized follow-up emails have a higher CLV.
- ✓ **Predictive Analytics**: You collaborate with a data scientist to develop a predictive model that forecasts future revenue based on lead qualification rates and lead response times.
- ✓ **Segmentation**: You segment your customer base by industry, company size, and geographic region. This segmentation helps your sales team customize their sales pitches and product recommendations.

In conclusion, sales metrics and analytics are invaluable tools for sales managers. By implementing the action plans and strategies outlined in this chapter, you can leverage data to measure performance, identify trends, and make data-driven decisions that enhance your sales team's effectiveness and drive results.

Sales Meetings and Communication

Effective communication within the sales team and conducting productive sales meetings are crucial for aligning goals, sharing information, and fostering collaboration. In this chapter, we'll explore strategies for achieving effective communication and optimizing your sales meetings.

Effective Communication within the Sales Team

- ✓ **Clear Communication Channels**: Establish clear and accessible communication channels for your team, such as email, chat tools, and project management software.
  Action Plan: Ensure that all team members have access to and are proficient in using these communication tools.
- ✓ **Regular Updates**: Encourage team members to provide regular updates on their progress, challenges, and successes.
  Action Plan: Implement a weekly or bi-weekly reporting system where team members share updates on their activities and results.
- ✓ **Active Listening**: Promote active listening within the team. Encourage team members to listen attentively to their colleagues and clients.
  Action Plan: Conduct training sessions on active listening techniques and encourage feedback that shows engagement and understanding.
- ✓ **Transparent Information Sharing**: Foster a culture of transparency by sharing important information about company performance, changes, and goals.

Action Plan: Schedule regular company-wide or team-wide meetings to share updates and ensure everyone is on the same page.

- ✓ **Feedback Mechanisms**: Establish feedback mechanisms that allow team members to provide constructive feedback to their peers and superiors.
  Action Plan: Implement a feedback tool or system where team members can offer feedback anonymously if needed.

Conducting Productive Sales Meetings

- ✓ **Set Clear Objectives**: Define the purpose and objectives of each sales meeting. What outcomes are you trying to achieve?
  Action Plan: Create an agenda that outlines meeting goals, topics, and expected outcomes.
- ✓ **Preparation**: Ensure that all participants come prepared. Distribute pre-meeting materials and information in advance.
  Action Plan: Send out meeting agendas and relevant documents at least a day before the meeting.
- ✓ **Time Management**: Stick to the allocated meeting time to avoid wasting participants' time. Use time management techniques to keep the meeting on track.
  Action Plan: Appoint a timekeeper or use timers to stay within the allotted time for each agenda item.
- ✓ **Engagement and Participation**: Encourage active participation from all team members. Create an inclusive environment where everyone feels comfortable sharing ideas and insights.

Action Plan: Assign roles to team members, such as a discussion leader or a note-taker, to ensure active participation.

- ✓ **Actionable Takeaways**: Ensure that each meeting results in actionable takeaways and clear next steps.

  Action Plan: Summarize key decisions and action items at the end of the meeting, and assign responsibilities.

Example: As a sales manager, you want to improve communication within your sales team and enhance the productivity of your sales meetings. Here's how you can implement these strategies:

- ✓ **Clear Communication Channels**: Standardize the use of a messaging app for quick communication among team members. Ensure that everyone is proficient in using the CRM system to log customer interactions and share relevant information.
- ✓ **Regular Updates**: Implement a weekly reporting system where each team member provides updates on their current pipeline, challenges they're facing, and wins they've had. Share these updates with the entire team.
- ✓ **Feedback Mechanisms**: Create an anonymous feedback system that allows team members to provide feedback on the effectiveness of meetings and communication channels. Use this feedback to make continuous improvements.
- ✓ **Conducting Productive Sales Meetings**: Before each meeting, circulate an agenda that outlines the meeting's objectives, such as reviewing sales targets, discussing recent

customer feedback, and sharing best practices.

- ✓ **Time Management**: Appoint a timekeeper for each meeting to ensure that discussions stay on track. Use a timer for agenda items to prevent them from running over the allocated time.
- ✓ **Actionable Takeaways**: Assign specific action items with deadlines at the end of each meeting. Follow up on these action items in the next meeting to track progress.

In conclusion, effective communication and productive sales meetings are essential for a successful sales team. By implementing the action plans and strategies outlined in this chapter, you can create an environment where open communication thrives, and meetings are a valuable tool for achieving your sales objectives.

Conflict Resolution and Problem Solving

Conflict resolution and problem-solving are essential skills for maintaining a harmonious sales team and overcoming challenges effectively. In this chapter, we'll explore strategies for resolving conflicts within the sales team and problem-solving techniques for sales managers.

Strategies for Resolving Conflicts within the Sales Team

- ✓ **Open Communication**: Encourage team members to communicate openly and honestly about their concerns and conflicts.
  Action Plan: Schedule regular one-on-one check-ins with team members to create a safe space for discussing conflicts.
- ✓ **Active Listening**: Train team members to actively listen to each other's perspectives without interrupting or making assumptions.
  Action Plan: Conduct workshops on active listening techniques and provide opportunities for team members to practice.
- ✓ **Mediation**: When conflicts arise, consider using a mediator, such as a senior salesperson or HR representative, to facilitate productive discussions and find resolutions.
  Action Plan: Train potential mediators within your team and establish a clear process for mediation when conflicts emerge.
- ✓ **Conflict Resolution Framework**: Develop a conflict resolution framework that outlines steps to follow when conflicts arise. This may

include identifying the issue, seeking common ground, and proposing solutions.
Action Plan: Create a step-by-step guide for handling conflicts and make it readily available to all team members.

- ✓ **Team Building Activities**: Organize team-building activities and workshops to strengthen team cohesion and address underlying interpersonal issues.
Action Plan: Schedule regular team-building sessions and encourage participation from all team members.

Problem-Solving Techniques for Sales Managers

- ✓ **Identify the Problem**: Clearly define the problem or challenge you're facing. What is the root cause of the issue?
Action Plan: Use problem-solving frameworks like the "5 Whys" technique to dig deeper into the underlying causes of a problem.
- ✓ **Gather Information**: Collect relevant data and information to understand the problem better. This may involve analyzing sales data, customer feedback, or market research.
Action Plan: Assign team members to gather data and conduct research on the problem.
- ✓ **Brainstorm Solutions**: Encourage your team to brainstorm potential solutions to the problem. Ensure that ideas are diverse and creative.
Action Plan: Organize brainstorming sessions where team members can freely share their ideas. Use techniques like mind mapping to visualize solutions.
- ✓ **Evaluate Solutions**: Assess the pros and cons of each solution. Consider their

feasibility, potential impact, and alignment with organizational goals.
Action Plan: Create a scoring system to evaluate solutions objectively, taking into account factors like cost, resources, and time.

- ✓ **Select a Solution**: Choose the most suitable solution based on your evaluation. Ensure that the selected solution addresses the root cause of the problem.
  Action Plan: Involve relevant stakeholders in the decision-making process to gain buy-in and support.
- ✓ **Implement and Monitor**: Develop an action plan for implementing the chosen solution. Assign responsibilities, set timelines, and continuously monitor progress.
  Action Plan: Create a project plan with clear milestones and regular check-ins to track progress.

Example: Suppose you're a sales manager facing a conflict between two members of your sales team, Sarah and Mike. They have been arguing over the allocation of leads, leading to tension and reduced collaboration. Here's how you can apply conflict resolution and problem-solving techniques:

- ✓ **Open Communication**: Arrange separate meetings with Sarah and Mike to allow each of them to express their concerns and perspectives on the lead allocation issue.
- ✓ **Mediation**: If the conflict persists, involve a senior salesperson or HR representative to mediate a discussion between Sarah and Mike, helping them find common ground.
- ✓ **Conflict Resolution Framework**: Develop a conflict resolution framework that includes a

step-by-step process for addressing conflicts within the team. Share this framework with all team members to promote a culture of conflict resolution.

- ✓ **Identify the Problem**: In another scenario, let's say your sales team is consistently falling short of their monthly sales targets. You use the "5 Whys" technique to uncover that the root cause is inadequate lead generation.
- ✓ **Gather Information**: Assign a team member to gather data on lead sources, conversion rates, and the quality of leads to get a comprehensive understanding of the lead generation problem.
- ✓ **Brainstorm Solutions**: Organize a brainstorming session with your team to generate ideas for improving lead generation. Ideas may include optimizing marketing campaigns, expanding the lead database, or refining lead qualification processes.
- ✓ **Evaluate Solutions**: Use a scoring system to objectively evaluate each solution. You determine that optimizing marketing campaigns and expanding the lead database are the most feasible and impactful options.
- ✓ **Select a Solution**: After obtaining buy-in from your team, you decide to prioritize optimizing marketing campaigns and allocate resources accordingly.
- ✓ **Implement and Monitor**: Create a detailed project plan for the optimization efforts, assign responsibilities, and schedule regular progress check-ins to ensure the solution is implemented effectively.

In conclusion, conflict resolution and problem-solving are essential skills for sales managers. By implementing the action plans and strategies outlined in this chapter, you can effectively address conflicts within your team and approach problem-solving with a structured and strategic mindset, leading to more successful outcomes.

Time Management and Productivity

Time management and productivity are critical for sales managers who must balance multiple responsibilities while leading their teams to success. In this chapter, we'll explore time management tips for sales managers and tools and strategies to enhance productivity.

Time Management Tips for Sales Managers

- ✓ **Prioritize Tasks**: Identify your most important tasks for the day or week and prioritize them. Focus on activities that have the most significant impact on your team's success.
  Action Plan: Start each day by creating a priority list and allocating dedicated time to high-impact tasks.
- ✓ **Time Blocking**: Allocate specific blocks of time for different types of tasks. For example, designate a block for team meetings, another for strategic planning, and one for individual coaching.
  Action Plan: Create a weekly time-blocking schedule that reflects your recurring activities and responsibilities.
- ✓ **Delegate Effectively**: Delegate tasks to your team members based on their strengths and capabilities. Trust your team to handle certain responsibilities, allowing you to focus on higher-priority tasks.
  Action Plan: Identify tasks that can be delegated and match them with team members who possess the necessary skills.
- ✓ **Avoid Multitasking**: Multitasking can decrease productivity and lead to errors.

Focus on one task at a time to improve efficiency and quality.

Action Plan: Implement a "single-tasking" approach by concentrating on completing one task before moving on to the next.

- ✓ **Set Boundaries**: Establish clear boundaries for your workday. Avoid over-committing to meetings and tasks that can disrupt your workflow.

  Action Plan: Communicate your availability and preferred meeting times to team members and colleagues.

Tools and Strategies to Enhance Productivity

- ✓ **Task Management Tools**: Use task management software or apps to track and organize your to-do list. Popular tools include Asana, Trello, or Todoist.

  Action Plan: Select a task management tool that suits your needs and integrate it into your daily workflow.
- ✓ **Automation**: Automate repetitive tasks wherever possible. For example, automate email responses, lead nurturing workflows, or data entry.

  Action Plan: Identify areas where automation can save you time and research software solutions that align with your automation needs.
- ✓ **Sales CRM**: A robust Customer Relationship Management (CRM) system can streamline sales processes, track leads, and manage customer data efficiently.

  Action Plan: Invest in a CRM platform that integrates seamlessly with your sales operations and provides advanced reporting and analytics.

- ✓ **Time Tracking Tools**: Use time tracking software to monitor how you spend your workday. This can help you identify time sinks and make necessary adjustments.
  Action Plan: Select a time tracking tool that suits your preferences and regularly review your time usage reports.
- ✓ **Collaboration and Communication Tools**: Leverage collaboration and communication tools like Slack, Microsoft Teams, or Zoom to facilitate efficient communication with your team.
  Action Plan: Train your team on how to use these tools effectively to streamline communication and reduce email overload.

Example: Imagine you're a sales manager for a pharmaceutical company, and you're struggling to balance your responsibilities effectively. You decide to implement time management and productivity strategies:

- ✓ **Prioritize Tasks**: You identify that coaching your sales team and analyzing sales data are your highest-impact tasks. You allocate dedicated time each morning for these activities.
- ✓ **Time Blocking**: You create a weekly time-blocking schedule that includes time for team meetings, strategic planning, and individual coaching sessions. This schedule ensures that you allocate time for each responsibility.
- ✓ **Delegation**: You delegate lead qualification tasks to a team member who excels in this

area. This frees up your time to focus on strategic planning and coaching.

- ✓ **Task Management Tool**: You start using a task management tool that allows you to organize your to-do list, set deadlines, and track your progress.
- ✓ **Automation**: You implement email automation for follow-up messages to leads, saving you time and ensuring that leads are nurtured effectively.
- ✓ **CRM System**: You invest in a CRM system that streamlines lead tracking, sales forecasting, and reporting, reducing manual data entry and improving data accuracy.
- ✓ **Time Tracking**: You use a time tracking tool to monitor your daily activities. This helps you identify areas where you can be more efficient and make necessary adjustments.
- ✓ **Collaboration Tools**: You encourage your team to use collaboration and communication tools for efficient communication and document sharing. This reduces the need for lengthy email exchanges.

By implementing these time management and productivity strategies and incorporating the selected tools, you optimize your workflow as a sales manager, allowing you to focus on strategic tasks, coach your team effectively, and drive outstanding results.

In conclusion, effective time management and productivity strategies are essential for sales managers to balance their responsibilities and lead their teams successfully. By incorporating the action plans and strategies outlined in this chapter, you can improve your efficiency, reduce time wasted on low-impact tasks, and ultimately achieve your sales objectives more effectively.

Customer Relationship Management

Customer Relationship Management (CRM) is a crucial aspect of sales management. In this chapter, we'll explore the role of CRM software in sales management and strategies for building and maintaining customer relationships.

The Role of CRM Software in Sales Management

CRM software plays a pivotal role in sales management by providing a centralized platform for managing customer information, interactions, and sales processes. Here's how CRM software contributes to effective sales management:

- ✓ **Centralized Customer Data**: CRM software gathers and stores comprehensive customer data, including contact information, communication history, purchase history, and preferences.

  Action Plan: Implement a CRM system that integrates seamlessly with your sales processes and ensures data accuracy.
- ✓ **Efficient Lead Management**: CRM systems help sales managers and representatives track leads throughout the sales pipeline, from initial contact to conversion.

  Action Plan: Create lead scoring models in your CRM to prioritize leads based on their likelihood to convert.
- ✓ **Sales Process Automation**: CRM software automates repetitive sales tasks, such as sending follow-up emails, appointment scheduling, and lead assignment.

Action Plan: Identify sales processes that can be automated and set up workflows within your CRM.

- ✓ **Sales Analytics**: CRM platforms offer advanced reporting and analytics features, allowing sales managers to gain insights into team performance, conversion rates, and sales trends.
  Action Plan: Regularly analyze CRM-generated reports to identify areas for improvement and make data-driven decisions.
- ✓ **Customer Segmentation**: CRM software enables the segmentation of customers based on various criteria, allowing for targeted marketing and personalized sales approaches.
  Action Plan: Create customer segments within your CRM based on factors like demographics, purchase history, or engagement level.
- ✓ **Pipeline Management**: CRM systems provide visual representations of the sales pipeline, making it easier to monitor progress, identify bottlenecks, and forecast sales.
  Action Plan: Implement pipeline management best practices, such as assigning stages to leads and setting clear criteria for each stage.

Building and Maintaining Customer Relationships

- ✓ **Personalization**: Tailor your interactions with customers to their preferences and needs. Address them by name, reference previous conversations, and offer relevant solutions.

Action Plan: Train your sales team to gather and use customer data effectively for personalization.

- ✓ **Active Listening**: Practice active listening during customer interactions. Allow customers to express their concerns and needs fully.
  Action Plan: Conduct training sessions on active listening techniques and provide opportunities for role-playing.
- ✓ **Regular Communication**: Maintain regular communication with customers, even when there are no immediate sales opportunities. Share valuable content, industry insights, or updates.
  Action Plan: Develop a customer communication schedule that includes periodic check-ins and valuable content sharing.
- ✓ **Feedback Collection**: Encourage customers to provide feedback on your products or services. Use their input to make improvements.
  Action Plan: Implement feedback collection mechanisms, such as surveys or feedback forms, and respond promptly to customer input.
- ✓ **Problem Resolution**: Address customer issues and complaints promptly and effectively. Show empathy and take responsibility for finding solutions.
  Action Plan: Train your team on effective problem-solving techniques and empower them to make decisions to resolve issues.

Example: Let's say you're a sales manager for a software company selling project management tools.

You've implemented CRM software to manage customer relationships effectively:

- ✓ **Centralized Customer Data**: Your CRM system stores detailed information about each customer, including their organization, role, and past interactions with your sales team.
- ✓ **Efficient Lead Management**: Your CRM tracks leads through the entire sales process. Leads are assigned scores based on their interactions with your website and email campaigns, ensuring that your sales team prioritizes the most promising prospects.
- ✓ **Sales Process Automation**: Your CRM automates follow-up emails and appointment scheduling. For example, when a lead requests a product demo on your website, the CRM automatically schedules a demo and sends reminders.
- ✓ **Sales Analytics**: You regularly review CRM-generated reports to assess your team's performance and identify areas for improvement. These reports help you allocate resources effectively and forecast future sales.
- ✓ **Customer Segmentation**: Within your CRM, you've created segments based on customer size (small businesses, enterprises), industry, and product usage. This allows your sales team to tailor their approach to each customer segment.

To build and maintain customer relationships:

- ✓ **Personalization**: Your sales team uses CRM data to personalize interactions with customers. For example, they reference a customer's industry-specific challenges during sales calls.

- ✓ **Active Listening**: Your team is trained in active listening techniques to understand customer needs fully and provide relevant solutions.
- ✓ **Regular Communication**: You've established a communication schedule where your team shares product updates, industry insights, and valuable content with customers through email newsletters and webinars.
- ✓ **Feedback Collection**: You use CRM surveys to collect customer feedback and suggestions for improving your product. When customers provide feedback, your team responds promptly with updates on how their input is being used to enhance the software.
- ✓ **Problem Resolution**: Your team is empowered to address customer issues immediately. They take ownership of problems and work collaboratively to find solutions, fostering trust and loyalty.

In conclusion, CRM software is a valuable tool for sales managers in managing customer relationships effectively. By implementing the action plans and strategies outlined in this chapter, you can leverage CRM technology to streamline sales processes, gain insights, and build strong, lasting customer relationships that drive sales success.

Sales Forecasting and Budgeting

Sales forecasting and budgeting are essential aspects of sales management that guide decision-making, resource allocation, and goal setting. In this chapter, we'll explore techniques for accurate sales forecasting and strategies for budgeting and resource allocation within the sales department.

Techniques for Accurate Sales Forecasting

- ✓ **Historical Data Analysis**: Review historical sales data, including revenue, conversion rates, and customer acquisition trends, to identify patterns and trends.
  Action Plan: Gather at least three years of historical data and use it as a basis for forecasting.
- ✓ **Sales Funnel Analysis**: Analyze the sales funnel to understand the conversion rates at each stage. This helps predict how many leads are likely to convert into customers.
  Action Plan: Use a CRM system to track leads and opportunities through the sales funnel and calculate conversion rates.
- ✓ **Market Research**: Conduct market research to assess industry trends, competitor performance, and potential market changes that could impact sales.
  Action Plan: Allocate a budget for market research or use industry reports and analysis tools.
- ✓ **Salesperson Input**: Collaborate with your sales team to gather insights and predictions based on their market knowledge and customer interactions.

Action Plan: Schedule regular forecasting meetings with your sales team to collect their input.

- ✓ **Qualitative and Quantitative Methods**: Combine quantitative methods (e.g., historical data analysis) with qualitative methods (e.g., expert opinions) for a more comprehensive forecast.
  Action Plan: Use quantitative data as a foundation and then adjust based on qualitative input.

Budgeting and Resource Allocation for the Sales Department

- ✓ **Set Clear Objectives**: Define specific sales objectives, such as revenue targets, market share goals, or new customer acquisition targets.
  Action Plan: Collaborate with your sales team to set achievable but challenging objectives that align with organizational goals.
- ✓ **Expense Analysis**: Review past sales department expenses and identify areas where cost optimization is possible.
  Action Plan: Conduct a detailed expense analysis, including sales team salaries, marketing costs, travel expenses, and software subscriptions.
- ✓ **Resource Allocation**: Allocate resources based on your sales objectives and forecasted sales. Consider investments in sales training, marketing campaigns, and lead generation.
  Action Plan: Create a resource allocation plan that specifies how funds and personnel will be distributed across different sales activities.

- ✓ **Contingency Planning**: Develop contingency plans in case actual sales fall short of the forecast. This might involve reallocating resources or adjusting expenses.
  Action Plan: Identify trigger points in your forecast at which you'll activate contingency plans.
- ✓ **Regular Monitoring**: Continuously monitor your budget and actual expenses. Make adjustments as needed to stay within budget while maintaining performance.
  Action Plan: Schedule regular budget review meetings to assess performance against the budget and make necessary revisions.

Example: Let's consider you're a sales manager for a retail clothing company, and you're preparing for the upcoming fiscal year. Here's how you can apply forecasting and budgeting strategies:

Sales Forecasting:

- ✓ **Historical Data Analysis**: You review the past three years of sales data and observe a consistent increase in sales during the holiday season.
- ✓ **Sales Funnel Analysis**: Your CRM system shows that the conversion rate from website visitors to customers has been steady at 5%. You expect this trend to continue.
- ✓ **Market Research**: You conduct market research and find that there is an increasing demand for eco-friendly clothing, which aligns with your product offerings.
- ✓ **Salesperson Input**: During a forecasting meeting with your sales team, they share insights that the introduction of a new loyalty

program has positively impacted customer retention.

- ✓ **Qualitative and Quantitative Methods**: Combining historical data, CRM insights, and market research, you forecast a 10% increase in sales for the upcoming year, with a significant boost during the holiday season.

Budgeting and Resource Allocation:

- ✓ **Set Clear Objectives**: You set a sales objective of achieving a 10% increase in revenue for the fiscal year, with a specific focus on holiday season promotions.
- ✓ **Expense Analysis**: You analyze past expenses and identify that reducing travel expenses for sales representatives by implementing virtual meetings can yield cost savings.
- ✓ **Resource Allocation**: Based on your sales forecast, you allocate additional funds for marketing campaigns during the holiday season and invest in sales training programs to enhance the skills of your team.
- ✓ **Contingency Planning**: You set a contingency plan in case actual sales fall short of the forecast. If sales remain flat or decrease, you'll reduce marketing expenses and review the sales team's performance.
- ✓ **Regular Monitoring**: You establish a quarterly budget review process to track expenses against the budget and make adjustments as necessary to ensure alignment with your sales objectives.

In conclusion, accurate sales forecasting and effective budgeting are vital for sales managers to plan and allocate resources efficiently. By implementing the action plans and strategies outlined in this chapter, you can make informed decisions, set realistic sales objectives, and manage your sales department's finances effectively to achieve outstanding results.

Managing Change and Adaptation

Change is a constant in the world of sales management. Whether it's adapting to industry changes, responding to market trends, or leading through organizational changes, sales managers must navigate and manage transitions effectively. In this chapter, we'll explore strategies for adapting to industry changes and leading through organizational changes.

Adapting to Industry Changes and Market Trends

- ✓ **Continuous Learning**: Foster a culture of continuous learning within your sales team. Encourage them to stay updated on industry trends, emerging technologies, and changing customer preferences.

  Action Plan: Organize regular training sessions, webinars, or workshops on industry developments and market trends.
- ✓ **Market Research**: Invest in market research to monitor shifts in customer behavior, preferences, and buying habits. Use this data to tailor your sales strategies.

  Action Plan: Allocate a budget for ongoing market research and analysis.
- ✓ **Competitive Analysis**: Keep a close eye on your competitors. Analyze their strategies, strengths, and weaknesses to identify opportunities and threats.

  Action Plan: Assign a team member or team to conduct regular competitive analyses and report findings.

- ✓ **Agile Sales Strategies**: Develop agile sales strategies that can be adjusted quickly in response to changing market conditions.
  Action Plan: Create a playbook of sales strategies that can be adapted or combined based on specific market scenarios.
- ✓ **Customer Feedback**: Actively seek feedback from customers to understand their evolving needs and expectations. Use this feedback to refine your product offerings and sales approach.
  Action Plan: Implement customer feedback surveys and conduct follow-up interviews to gather insights.

Leading Through Organizational Changes

- ✓ **Clear Communication**: During times of organizational change, maintain clear and transparent communication with your sales team. Explain the reasons for the change, its impact, and the expected outcomes.
  Action Plan: Schedule regular meetings or town halls to address questions and concerns.
- ✓ **Change Champions**: Identify change champions within your team who can help facilitate the transition and inspire others. These individuals can serve as role models for embracing change.
  Action Plan: Appoint change champions and involve them in planning and communication efforts.
- ✓ **Change Management Plan**: Develop a structured change management plan that outlines the steps, timeline, and responsibilities for implementing the change.

Action Plan: Create a detailed change management plan that includes key milestones and success indicators.

- ✓ **Employee Training**: Ensure that your team has the necessary skills and knowledge to adapt to new processes or technologies. Provide training and resources to support their development.
  Action Plan: Organize training sessions and workshops that align with the change initiative.
- ✓ **Feedback Mechanisms**: Establish feedback mechanisms that allow team members to share their concerns, suggestions, and experiences related to the change.
  Action Plan: Set up regular feedback sessions, anonymous suggestion boxes, or digital feedback channels.

Example: Suppose you're a sales manager for a tech company, and you're facing industry changes related to a shift in customer preferences for cloud-based solutions over traditional on-premises software. Additionally, your organization is implementing a major change in its pricing model. Here's how you can apply strategies for adapting to industry changes and leading through organizational changes:

Adapting to Industry Changes and Market Trends:

- ✓ **Continuous Learning**: You organize monthly webinars where your team learns about the latest trends in cloud technology and customer preferences for subscription-based models.
- ✓ **Market Research**: You allocate a budget to hire a market research firm to analyze

customer buying habits and preferences for cloud solutions.

- ✓ **Competitive Analysis**: Your team conducts a competitive analysis to identify which competitors are successfully adapting to cloud trends and how they are doing it.
- ✓ **Agile Sales Strategies**: You create an agile sales playbook that includes strategies for selling both cloud and on-premises solutions, with the flexibility to adjust focus based on market demand.
- ✓ **Customer Feedback**: You launch a customer feedback survey focused on understanding their cloud solution needs and gather valuable insights for product development.

Leading Through Organizational Changes:

- ✓ **Clear Communication**: You schedule a series of town hall meetings to communicate the reasons behind the pricing model change, its benefits, and the impact on the sales team.
- ✓ **Change Champions**: You identify team members who have experience with subscription-based models and ask them to lead training sessions for the rest of the team.
- ✓ **Change Management Plan**: You create a detailed change management plan that outlines the steps for transitioning to the new pricing model, including training, customer communication, and sales team support.
- ✓ **Employee Training**: You organize training sessions to ensure that your team is proficient in selling the new pricing model and can answer customer questions confidently.
- ✓ **Feedback Mechanisms**: You set up regular feedback sessions where team members can

voice their concerns and suggestions regarding the pricing model change. You also establish an anonymous suggestion box for additional input.

In conclusion, managing change and adaptation is a crucial skill for sales managers. By implementing the action plans and strategies outlined in this chapter, you can effectively lead your team through industry changes and organizational transitions, ensuring that your sales strategies remain aligned with evolving market trends and customer needs.

Ethics and Compliance

Ethics and compliance are foundational principles in sales management. This chapter delves into the importance of ethical sales practices and how to ensure compliance with legal and industry standards.

The Importance of Ethical Sales Practices

- ✓ **Customer Trust and Reputation**: Ethical sales practices build trust with customers and enhance your company's reputation. Customers are more likely to do business with companies they perceive as honest and trustworthy.
  Action Plan: Emphasize the importance of trust-building in sales training programs and internal communications.
- ✓ **Long-Term Relationships**: Ethical sales practices focus on building long-term customer relationships rather than short-term gains. This can result in repeat business and customer loyalty.
  Action Plan: Encourage your sales team to prioritize customer relationships over quick sales wins.
- ✓ **Legal and Regulatory Compliance**: Ethical practices ensure your sales team operates within the bounds of the law and complies with industry regulations. Violating ethical guidelines can lead to legal repercussions.
  Action Plan: Provide regular training on legal and regulatory requirements relevant to your industry.
- ✓ **Employee Morale and Engagement**: A commitment to ethical practices boosts

employee morale and engagement. When employees believe they work for an ethical company, they are more likely to be motivated and proud of their work.
Action Plan: Promote ethical behavior through company culture and leadership example.

- ✓ **Risk Mitigation**: Ethical sales practices reduce the risk of lawsuits, fines, and damage to the company's brand reputation that may result from unethical behavior.
Action Plan: Develop clear policies and procedures related to ethics and compliance, and ensure all employees are aware of and follow them.

Ensuring Compliance with Legal and Industry Standards

- ✓ **Policy Development**: Develop comprehensive ethics and compliance policies that outline the expected behavior of your sales team. These policies should cover legal requirements, industry regulations, and ethical standards.
Action Plan: Collaborate with legal experts to draft and review your company's ethics and compliance policies.
- ✓ **Training and Education**: Conduct regular training sessions to educate your sales team about ethics, compliance, and legal requirements. Ensure they understand the implications of non-compliance.
Action Plan: Create a training calendar that includes ethics and compliance training modules and refresher courses.
- ✓ **Ethics Hotline**: Implement an ethics hotline or reporting mechanism that allows employees to

report unethical behavior confidentially. Encourage employees to use this channel without fear of retaliation.

Action Plan: Prominently advertise the ethics hotline and ensure anonymity and confidentiality for those who report concerns.

- ✓ **Auditing and Monitoring**: Regularly audit sales processes and transactions to identify potential compliance issues. Use data analytics to detect irregularities.

  Action Plan: Establish a dedicated compliance team or hire external auditors to perform regular audits.

- ✓ **Consequences for Non-Compliance**: Clearly communicate the consequences of non-compliance with ethics and compliance policies. Ensure that violations are dealt with swiftly and fairly.

  Action Plan: Develop a disciplinary process that includes warnings, retraining, and, if necessary, termination for serious violations.

Example: Imagine you're a sales manager for a pharmaceutical company, and your team is responsible for promoting prescription medications to healthcare professionals. Here's how you can apply ethical practices and ensure compliance with legal and industry standards:

The Importance of Ethical Sales Practices:

- ✓ **Customer Trust and Reputation**: You emphasize to your sales team that they must provide accurate and balanced information about your medications, including potential side effects, to healthcare professionals. You stress the importance of transparency in building trust.

- ✓ **Long-Term Relationships**: You encourage your team to focus on building long-term relationships with healthcare professionals by offering ongoing support and education rather than pushing for quick prescriptions.

Ensuring Compliance with Legal and Industry Standards:

- ✓ **Policy Development**: You collaborate with your company's legal department to develop comprehensive compliance policies that align with pharmaceutical regulations. These policies include guidelines on interactions with healthcare professionals and adherence to the Pharmaceutical Code.
- ✓ **Training and Education**: You conduct regular training sessions that cover ethical considerations, legal requirements, and industry regulations. For instance, you provide training on the an Act, which requires reporting of financial interactions with healthcare professionals.
- ✓ **Ethics Hotline**: Your company maintains an ethics hotline that allows employees to report any concerns or potential violations confidentially. You communicate the availability of this hotline to your team and assure them of confidentiality.
- ✓ **Auditing and Monitoring**: You periodically audit interactions and communications with healthcare professionals to ensure compliance with regulatory requirements. You also use data analytics to identify any unusual or non-compliant patterns.
- ✓ **Consequences for Non-Compliance**: You have a clear disciplinary process in place.

Minor violations may result in retraining, while serious violations are subject to investigation and, if necessary, disciplinary action.

In conclusion, ethical sales practices and compliance with legal and industry standards are paramount in sales management, especially in regulated industries like pharmaceuticals. By implementing the action plans and strategies outlined in this chapter, you can create a culture of ethics and compliance within your sales team, leading to increased customer trust, long-term success, and risk mitigation.

Personal Development for Sales Managers

Personal development and maintaining a healthy work-life balance are crucial for sales managers to thrive in their roles and lead their teams effectively. In this chapter, we'll explore the importance of personal growth and work-life balance and provide strategies to achieve them.

Personal Growth and Self-Improvement for Sales Managers

- ✓ **Continuous Learning**: Recognize that personal growth is an ongoing process. Commit to continuous learning by staying updated on sales trends, leadership strategies, and management techniques.
  Action Plan: Allocate time each week for reading industry-related books, attending webinars, or enrolling in relevant courses.
- ✓ **Self-Reflection**: Regularly reflect on your performance as a sales manager. Identify areas where you can improve your leadership skills, communication, and decision-making.
  Action Plan: Set aside time for self-assessment and consider seeking feedback from peers or mentors.
- ✓ **Goal Setting**: Define clear personal and professional goals. These goals should align with your career aspirations and areas where you want to grow.
  Action Plan: Create a list of short-term and long-term goals, both personally and professionally. Review and update them regularly.

- ✓ **Networking**: Build and maintain a strong professional network. Connect with colleagues, mentors, and industry peers who can provide guidance and support.
  Action Plan: Attend industry conferences, join professional associations, and participate in online networking communities.
- ✓ **Mentorship**: Seek out a mentor or coach who can provide guidance and share their experiences. A mentor can offer valuable insights and help you navigate challenges.
  Action Plan: Identify potential mentors within your organization or industry and approach them for mentorship.

Strategies for Maintaining Work-Life Balance

- ✓ **Set Boundaries**: Establish clear boundaries between work and personal life. Define specific working hours and avoid answering work-related emails or calls during personal time.
  Action Plan: Communicate your boundaries to your team and colleagues and request respect for your personal time.
- ✓ **Prioritize Self-Care**: Make self-care a priority. This includes maintaining a healthy lifestyle through exercise, a balanced diet, and adequate sleep.
  Action Plan: Schedule regular exercise sessions and prioritize a healthy diet and sufficient sleep.
- ✓ **Time Management**: Efficiently manage your time to minimize work-related stress. Use time management techniques like time blocking and prioritizing tasks.

Action Plan: Implement time management strategies to optimize your daily schedule.

- ✓ **Delegate Responsibilities**: Delegate tasks to your team members and empower them to take ownership of their roles. Avoid micromanaging, which can lead to burnout.
  Action Plan: Identify tasks that can be delegated and match them with team members' strengths and capabilities.
- ✓ **Unplug Regularly**: Take regular breaks from technology and work-related screens. Disconnecting allows you to recharge and reduce stress.
  Action Plan: Schedule technology-free periods, such as evenings or weekends, for relaxation and family time.

Example: Suppose you're a sales manager for a software company, and you're juggling a demanding role while striving for personal growth and work-life balance. Here's how you can apply these principles:

Personal Growth and Self-Improvement:

- ✓ **Continuous Learning**: You set aside an hour each morning to read sales management books, industry news, and leadership articles.
- ✓ **Self-Reflection**: Every quarter, you conduct a self-assessment, noting areas where you can improve your team's performance and your leadership style.
- ✓ **Goal Setting**: You define clear goals, including achieving a 20% increase in team productivity over the next year and improving your coaching skills.
- ✓ **Networking**: You attend an industry conference and join an online sales manager

community to connect with peers and gain insights.

- ✓ **Mentorship**: You reach out to a senior sales manager within your organization and ask them to mentor you on strategic leadership.

Strategies for Maintaining Work-Life Balance:

- ✓ **Set Boundaries**: You communicate your working hours to your team and refrain from responding to emails or calls after 7 p.m.
- ✓ **Prioritize Self-Care**: You schedule regular workouts and prioritize a balanced diet and 7-8 hours of sleep each night.
- ✓ **Time Management**: You implement time-blocking techniques to ensure dedicated personal time and prioritize tasks that align with your goals.
- ✓ **Delegate Responsibilities**: You delegate some of your team's administrative tasks to team members, empowering them to take ownership.
- ✓ **Unplug Regularly**: You dedicate weekends to technology-free activities, spending quality time with your family, and engaging in hobbies.

In conclusion, personal development and maintaining a healthy work-life balance are essential for sales managers to thrive in their roles and lead effectively. By implementing the action plans and strategies outlined in this chapter, you can continually improve your skills, achieve your goals, and ensure a fulfilling work-life balance.

A Detailed Action Plan for Sales Managers to put these Skills into Practice

Creating a detailed action plan for a Sales Manager to put various skills into practice involves organizing tasks, setting goals, and executing strategies. Below is a comprehensive action plan with strategies and examples to guide a Sales Manager in implementing these skills effectively into their routine.

Action Plan for a Sales Manager

Week 1-2: Strategic Leadership and Team Building

Objective: Establish a clear vision, build a cohesive team, and set the tone for professional growth.

Week 1:

Leadership Vision:

Strategy: Define a clear leadership vision that aligns with company goals.

Example: Develop a vision statement emphasizing customer-centricity and continuous improvement.

Team Building:

Strategy: Schedule a team-building session.

Example: Host a team-building workshop focusing on trust-building exercises and communication.

Week 2:

Leadership Communication:

Strategy: Communicate the leadership vision to the team.

Example: Conduct a team meeting to share the vision statement and invite feedback.

Team Engagement:
Strategy: Encourage individual goal setting.
Example: Ask team members to define their career goals and how they align with department objectives.

Week 3-4: Sales Training and Performance Management
Objective: Equip the team with necessary skills and implement performance monitoring.

Week 3:
Sales Training Program:
Strategy: Research and select a suitable sales training program.
Example: Partner with a sales training organization to provide customized training sessions.
Performance Metrics:
Strategy: Define key performance indicators (KPIs).
Example: Set KPIs, such as conversion rates, for each team member.

Week 4:
Training Implementation:
Strategy: Launch the sales training program.
Example: Conduct the first training session, focusing on objection handling.
Performance Reviews:
Strategy: Schedule one-on-one performance reviews.
Example: Meet with team members to assess their progress against KPIs and provide constructive feedback.

Month 2-3: Data-Driven Decision-Making and Ethics

Objective: Embrace data-driven insights and ensure ethical sales practices.

\Month 2:

Data Analytics Tools:

Strategy: Implement data analytics tools.

Example: Integrate CRM software to track customer interactions and sales data.

Ethical Guidelines:

Strategy: Develop and distribute a code of ethics.

Example: Create a document outlining ethical sales practices, such as transparent pricing and honest communication.

Month 3:

Data Analysis:

Strategy: Analyze sales data to identify trends.

Example: Analyze sales data to discover which products have the highest and lowest conversion rates.

Ethics Training:

Strategy: Conduct ethics training sessions.

Example: Invite an ethics expert to provide training on ethical decision-making in sales scenarios.

Month 4-5: Personal Development and Work-Life Balance

Objective: Foster personal growth and maintain a healthy work-life balance.

\Month 4:

Personal Growth Plan:

Strategy: Create a personal development plan.

Example: Set a goal to read one sales-related book per month.

Work-Life Boundaries:
Strategy: Establish clear work-life boundaries.
Example: Dedicate evenings and weekends to personal time and family.

Month 5:
Continued Learning:
Strategy: Attend industry conferences or webinars.
Example: Register for a sales leadership conference to gain insights into industry trends.
Self-Care Routine:
Strategy: Prioritize self-care activities.
Example: Dedicate 30 minutes each morning to meditation or exercise.

Month 6: Networking and Feedback
Objective: Expand your professional network and seek continuous improvement.
Networking Events:
Strategy: Attend networking events.
Example: Join an industry-specific LinkedIn group and engage in discussions.
Feedback Culture:
Strategy: Promote a feedback-friendly environment.
Example: Conduct a team survey to gather feedback on your leadership style and areas for improvement.

By following this six-month action plan, Sales Managers can systematically develop and apply the essential skills needed for success in their role. It combines leadership, team building, sales training, data analysis, ethics, personal development, work-life balance, networking, and feedback into a structured routine that fosters growth and drives results.

Templates and Resources for Sales Planning, Performance Evaluation, and More

Here are some examples of templates and resources for various aspects of sales management, along with detailed steps of action plans and strategies for their effective use:

1. Sales Planning Template:

Action Plan: Create a comprehensive sales planning template that includes sections for setting objectives, defining strategies, and outlining tactics. This template should align with your organizational goals.

Strategy: Break down the sales planning process into specific steps:

- ✓ **Define Objectives**: Clearly state your sales goals and objectives for the coming quarter or year.
- ✓ **Market Analysis**: Conduct thorough market research to understand trends, competition, and potential opportunities.
- ✓ **Target Audience**: Identify your ideal customer personas and create a profile for your target audience.
- ✓ **Sales Strategies**: Develop strategies for reaching your target audience, such as through content marketing, advertising, or direct sales efforts.
- ✓ **Tactical Plans**: Outline specific tactics for each strategy, including timelines and responsible team members.

- ✓ **Budget Allocation**: Allocate budget resources to each tactic, ensuring that your plan is financially viable.

Execution: Implement your sales planning template with regular reviews and updates to adapt to changing circumstances.

2. Performance Evaluation Scorecard:

Action Plan: Create a performance evaluation scorecard to assess individual and team performance against key performance indicators (KPIs).

Strategy:

- ✓ **Identify Key Metrics**: Determine the essential KPIs for your sales team, such as conversion rates, revenue per salesperson, or customer retention rates.
- ✓ **Scorecard Creation**: Design a scorecard that includes these metrics and provides a clear method for scoring performance.
- ✓ **Regular Evaluation**: Set a schedule for regular performance evaluations, such as quarterly or annually.
- ✓ **Feedback Mechanism**: Include a section for providing feedback and coaching to help team members improve.

Execution: Use the performance evaluation scorecard during regular one-on-one meetings with team members to provide feedback, identify areas for improvement, and set performance improvement goals.

3. Sales Playbook:

Action Plan: Develop a comprehensive sales playbook that serves as a resource for your sales team, providing guidance on processes, best practices, and objection handling.

Strategy:

- ✓ **Content Creation**: Create content for the playbook, including sales scripts, objection handling guides, product knowledge, and competitive analysis.
- ✓ **Training**: Use the playbook as part of your training program to onboard new team members and continuously update existing ones.
- ✓ **Sales Processes**: Document your sales processes, from lead generation to closing deals, in a clear and step-by-step manner.
- ✓ **Objection Handling**: Include common objections and strategies for handling them effectively.

Execution: Distribute the sales playbook to your team and encourage them to use it as a reference during their daily sales activities. Regularly update the playbook to reflect changes in your industry and products.

4. Sales Forecasting Spreadsheet:

Action Plan: Create a sales forecasting spreadsheet to project future sales based on historical data and current trends.

Strategy:

- ✓ **Data Collection**: Gather historical sales data, market research, and insights from your team.
- ✓ **Forecasting Model**: Develop a forecasting model that incorporates this data and takes into account variables like seasonality and market fluctuations.

- ✓ **Regular Updates**: Update the spreadsheet regularly, preferably on a monthly or quarterly basis, to refine your forecasts as new information becomes available.
- ✓ **Scenario Planning**: Include multiple scenarios in your spreadsheet, such as best-case, worst-case, and most likely scenarios, to prepare for various outcomes.

Execution: Use the sales forecasting spreadsheet to inform your sales strategy, budget allocation, and resource planning. Compare actual sales to your forecasts to refine your forecasting model over time.

5. CRM Software:

Action Plan: Implement Customer Relationship Management (CRM) software to streamline customer data management, track interactions, and improve sales processes.

Strategy:

- ✓ **Selection**: Choose a CRM system that aligns with your organization's needs and integrates with your existing tools.
- ✓ **Training**: Provide comprehensive training to your team on how to use the CRM effectively.
- ✓ **Data Management**: Establish protocols for data entry, data cleaning, and data security within the CRM.
- ✓ **Automation**: Utilize automation features to streamline tasks such as lead nurturing and follow-ups.

Execution: Integrate the CRM software into your daily operations, ensuring that all team members use it consistently for customer relationship management.

These templates and resources, when integrated into your sales management processes, can enhance your team's efficiency, effectiveness, and overall performance. Regularly review and update them to stay aligned with your organizational goals and industry trends.

Conclusion

In this comprehensive guide on '**Mastering Sales Managerial Skills**: *Building High-Performing Teams & Driving Exceptional Results'* we've navigated a vast landscape of knowledge, strategies, and best practices essential for success in the dynamic and ever-evolving realm of sales management. As our journey together comes to a close, it's essential to revisit and reflect on the key takeaways, reinforce the importance of continuous learning and development, and provide you with actionable steps for your ongoing growth as a Sales Manager.

Key Takeaways:

- ✓ **Strategic Leadership**: As a Sales Manager, adopting a strategic leadership approach is paramount. Focus on long-term goals, customer-centricity, and a culture of continuous improvement.

  Action Plan: Set aside dedicated time each quarter for strategic planning and goal setting with your team.
- ✓ **Team Building**: Building a cohesive sales team is crucial. Effective leadership, open communication, and fostering a positive team culture lead to higher performance.

  Action Plan: Conduct regular team-building activities and encourage open communication within your team.
- ✓ **Sales Training and Development**: Invest in comprehensive sales training programs and continuous learning to equip your team with the skills needed to excel.

Action Plan: Allocate a portion of your budget to ongoing sales training and development initiatives.

- ✓ **Performance Management**: Regularly assess individual and team performance, provide constructive feedback and coaching to drive improvement.
  Action Plan: Implement a performance review process with clear KPIs and developmental goals.
- ✓ **Data-Driven Decision-Making**: Embrace data analytics to make informed sales decisions, track progress, and adjust strategies as needed.
  Action Plan: Integrate data analytics tools into your sales processes and regularly review performance metrics.
- ✓ **Ethics and Compliance**: Uphold the highest ethical standards and ensure compliance with legal and industry regulations to build trust with customers and protect your organization.
  Action Plan: Continuously educate your team on ethics and compliance requirements and regularly audit processes for adherence.
- ✓ **Personal Development**: Prioritize personal growth as a Sales Manager. Continuous learning, self-reflection, and goal setting are key to your success.
  Action Plan: Set aside time each week for self-improvement activities and reflection.
- ✓ **Work-Life Balance**: Maintain a healthy work-life balance to prevent burnout and enhance your overall well-being.

Action Plan: Establish clear boundaries between work and personal life, and regularly schedule downtime for self-care.

Encouraging Ongoing Learning and Development:

- ✓ **Never Stop Learning**: Commit to lifelong learning by staying updated on industry trends, leadership best practices, and emerging technologies.
  Action Plan: Dedicate at least an hour each week to reading industry literature or participating in relevant webinars.
- ✓ **Networking**: Build and nurture your professional network by connecting with mentors, peers, and industry experts who can offer guidance and support.
  Action Plan: Attend industry events, join online networking groups, and seek out mentors.
- ✓ **Mentorship**: Consider both being a mentor and finding a mentor. Mentorship is a two-way street that benefits both parties.
  Action Plan: Identify potential mentees within your team and offer guidance. Simultaneously, seek out a mentor who can provide valuable insights.
- ✓ **Feedback and Adaptation**: Continuously seek feedback from your team, colleagues, and superiors. Use this feedback to adapt your leadership style and strategies.
  Action Plan: Create a feedback-friendly environment and regularly solicit input from your team.
- ✓ **Training Programs**: Invest in training programs not only for your team but also for

yourself. Attend courses, workshops, and seminars to stay current and develop new skills.

Action Plan: Allocate a portion of your budget and schedule time for personal training and development.

Moving Forward:

As you move forward in your role as a Sales Manager, remember that excellence in sales management is an ongoing journey. The strategies and skills you've acquired from this book provide a strong foundation, but to truly excel, you must embrace a growth mindset and continue evolving.

Your commitment to strategic leadership, team building, data-driven decision-making, ethical practices, personal development, and maintaining a work-life balance will not only elevate your own success but also empower your sales team to achieve outstanding results. By fostering a culture of learning and development within your team, you'll create a dynamic and resilient sales force capable of adapting to changing market conditions and driving your organization's growth.

In the ever-evolving world of sales, your dedication to growth and excellence will be your greatest asset. Embrace the challenges, seize the opportunities, and continue your journey toward becoming an exceptional Sales Manager. Your success is not just a destination; it's a continuous path of improvement and achievement.

The path you've chosen as a Sales Manager is an honorable one, filled with opportunities to make a profound impact on your team, your organization, and your own professional journey. As you embark on this path, remember that the commitment to continuous growth and development will be your guiding light, illuminating the way to remarkable success.

About the Author 'GERARD ASSEY'

Gerard Assey is a Graduate in Economics, a PGD in Management (HRD) and holds a Doctorate in Leadership. Gerard holds several International Qualifications in Sales, Debt Collection, Training & Teaching, and is a 'Fellow' of the prestigious 'Institute of Sales & Marketing Management'-UK, a Certified NLP Practitioner, a 'Certified Trainer', an 'Accredited Management Teacher-Behavioral Sciences', a 'Certified Competency Facilitator', a 'Certified Management Consultant'- (the International credentials of a professional management consultant, awarded in accordance with global standards of the ICMCI); and a Certification from the University of Michigan in 'Successful Negotiation: Essential Strategies and Skills'

He is also a Member of the 'National Association of Sales Professionals' backed with several years experience in varied industries, both in India and Overseas. He also holds an 'Etiquette Consultant' Certification from the USA (by Sue Fox, Author of Best Seller: 'Business Etiquette for Dummies'. She has trained some of the top celebrities' world over). He was also a recipient of a scholarship for extensive training in Japan on 'Corporate Management for India'.

Gerard Assey is 'Founder & Chief Corporate Trainer' of the Group: '**Citius, Altius, Fortius Unlimited**'- an organization that **celebrated 20 years of Glorious Service** in 2021, focusing on 3 Core Competencies:

People. Performance. Profit; in functional areas of Sales & Marketing, HR & Organizational Development, covering Recruitment, Training & Consultancy!

Having managed organizations with large Sales Forces in India & Overseas, his specialization cover extensive areas of Sales Training (All levels - Presentation, Negotiation, Key/ Strategic Accounts Management & Managerial Skills for all sectors), Bid Proposal/ Capture Planning/ Management Trainings, Retail Sales, Customer Service & Customer Retention Programs, Training for Prevention & Collection of Debt, Self & Personal Development Programs (Time Management, Teamwork & Team Building, Business Etiquette & Personal Grooming, Leadership & Managerial Skills, People Management Skills, Train-the-Trainer etc), including preparation of Custom-designed Business Manuals for Internal (HR, Induction, and Sales etc) & External use (Instruction, User Manuals).

Gerard has successfully conducted over 6050 Trainings & Workshops (as of Jan '24) all across India, Middle East, Africa, Europe & S.E. Asia. Besides public programs conducted regularly, both in India & Overseas, he has some of the top names as clients whom he services from Single Owners to large Public & Government undertakings, covering all sectors, for their in-house needs.

His website: www.CollectionSkills.com is the only one in this part of the world to be featured in the 'Collections & Credit Risk Magazine-USA' under 'Who's Who in Training' and ranks TOP, along with other websites listed below on most search engines.

Gerard is author of 107 books already (Jan 2024)

A few of our business related books:

1. Bite-sized Bits on Commonsense Management
2. Heart to Heart on Life's Principles'
3. How to become a Successful Manager
4. The Sales Professionals' Master Workbook of S.Y.S.T.E.M.S
5. The Professional Business Email Etiquette Handbook & Guide
6. The Professional Business Video-Conferencing Etiquette Handbook & Guide
7. Professional Presentation Skills
8. Exceptional Customer Service
9. Professional Tele-Marketing Skills
10. Professional Debt Collection Skills
11. The G.R.E.A.T. Sales & Service Workbook
12. Sales Training Advantage for Results (*The Ultimate Sales Training Manual to enable you stand out as a S.T.A.R.*)
13. CEO Daily Planner & Organizer
14. The Sales Professionals' Master Daily Planner
15. The Professional Debt Collector's Master Daily Planner
16. My Daily Planner & Organizer
17. MY EMERGENCY INFORMATION RECORD (Family Emergency & Peace of Mind Planner)
18. The Ultimate Therapist & Counselors Planner and Organizer
19. Building an Ethical Workplace
20. Managing Relationships at Work
21. Managing Business Meetings Effectively
22. Effective Delegation Skills
23. Goal Setting for Success
24. B2B Selling by Email
25. Professional Business Etiquette & Grooming
26. Dining Etiquette & Table Manners
27. Effective Networking Skills
28. Grooming, Etiquette & Manners for Teens, Young Adults & Future Leaders
29. Inter-Personal Skills
30. Get Ready, Get Hired!
31. Selling in a Recession
32. Effective Receivables Management in an Economic Downturn!
33. Real Estate & Property Sales Training
34. Credit Sales & Accounts Receivable Management
35. Selling Skills for Real Estate & Property Advisors
36. Take G.R.E.A.T. C.A.R.E!
37. Spa, Salon & Health Club Selling Skills
38. Selling Travel, Holiday & MICE Services
39. Selling Skills for Spa's, Salons & Health Clubs
40. Retailing in Salons & Spas

41. Selling Holiday, Vacation, Tours & Packages
42. The Power of Sales Referrals
43. Selling Luxury
44. Technical Selling Skills
45. Financial Advisors Sales Training
46. Dealing with Burnout at Work Monopolize Your Markets
47. Selling to Affluent Customers
48. Growing up with Grace
49. Financial Selling Skills
50. *The Effective Manager's Guide: Key Skills to Thrive*
51. From Aspiring to Inspiring: A Guide for New Managers on the Rise
52. The Power of Focus
53. Selling with Integrity: Sell Like Jesus The Perfect Role Model!
54. 31 Habits of Champions: Your 31-Day Journey to Greatness
55. Rejecting Grasshopper Talk: From Grasshopper to Giant-Killer-*Defeating Giants Daily!*
56. Navigate the AI-Powered Future of Bid & Proposals: Up-Skill to Stay Relevant with Alternative Career Paths & Opportunities
57. Hiring Sales Winners
58. Present with Impact
59. Success Unlocked: *Breaking Free from Habits that Hold You Back*
60. Complaints to Cheers, Feedback to Gold: Mastering Complaints Management
61. Thriving Together: *Cultivating Diversity, Equity, and Inclusion*
62. Coaching Skills for Sales Managers
63. Soaring to Success in Business & Leadership: Swifter, Higher, Stronger!
64. From Classroom to Podium: A Student's Guide to Powerful Public Speaking & Presentation Skills
65. Developing Self-Discipline
66. The CEO's 31-Day Power Plan: Unlocking Success through Essential Traits
67. Credibility Matters
68. A Winning Attitude
69. Bid & Proposal Management Using AI
70. Sales Forecasting: A Practical & Proven Guide to Strategic Sales Forecasting
71. Elevate & Energize: *50 Dynamic & Fun Activities for Peak Workplace Morale*
72. 'Sales SOS! Sales on Fire! *30 Days to Conquer Chaos & the Nightmares of Success!'*
73. Mastering Sales Managerial Skills: *Building High-Performing Teams & Driving Exceptional Results*

Besides regularly contributing to business & trade journals, including international ones such as the 'Creative Training Techniques' and the 'Sales News' of the U.S.A, He is also a member of several prestigious bodies & trade associations, having participated in many Conferences & Workshops in India & Overseas.

Prior to his last assignment of leading & managing a large MNC as head, Gerard had a 3-year stint in the Middle East as a Consultant with a leading British Consultancy Firm.

As the past 'Official Country Representative' for the International Business Award- 'THE STEVIES'-(the business world's own Oscar) for about 4 years- he ensured a few Indian companies that qualify for the same every year!

Gerard can be contacted at:
Email: training@Sales-Training.in,training@CollectionSkills.com
Websites:

www.Sales-Training.in
www.EtiquetteWorks.in
www.CollectionSkills.com
www.RetailSalesTraining.in
www.SalesTrainingIndia.com
www.ManualPreparation.com
www.TrainingWithPuppets.com
www.FirstContactAcademy.com
www.SalesAndMarketingRecruiter.com

Our TRAININGS that can help your team

- ✓ **Sales Effectiveness**: Selling Skills for any Sector: Service/ Logistics/ FMCG Realty/ Insurance & Finance/ Media/ SPA's, Health Clubs & Salons/ Key Account Management, Effective Negotiation Skills/ Bid & Proposal Management Skills/ Retail Sales Training: Any Sector (Auto, Jewelry, Clothing, Luxury etc)
- ✓ **Customer Service Skills**-Complaints Handling & Customer Retention
- ✓ **Debt Prevention & Collection Skills**
- ✓ **Etiquette & Grooming**
- ✓ **Leadership & Managerial Skills**
- ✓ **Self & Personal Development Skills**: Presentation Skills/ Effective Communication Skills/Business Proposal Writing Skills/ Problem Solving & Decision Making Skills/ Empowering Secretaries-The perfect PA! (For Secretaries & PA's)/ Effective Time Management/ Teamwork & Teambuilding/ P.R.I.D.E- **P**ersonal **R**esponsibility **I**n **D**elivering **E**xcellence

www.ingramcontent.com/pod-product-compliance
Lightning Source LLC
Chambersburg PA
CBHW062110160726
48282CB00026B/743
* 9 7 8 9 3 9 2 4 9 2 9 4 5 *